"This book gives abundant, practical findings and insights with emphasis on how to develop EQ. Research shows convincingly that EQ is more important than IQ in almost every role and many times more important in leadership roles."

—Stephen R. Covey, author of the perennial bestseller, *The 7 Habits of Highly Effective People*

"Emotional intelligence is an extremely important skill to have for personal and professional success. This book is excellent and the learning included in the free online test is cutting-edge. I strongly recommend it."

—Ken Blanchard, bestselling business book author of all time; coauthor of *The One Minute Manager*®

"My clients tend to be very successful and incredibly busy. This book delivers valuable insights without wasting time! My coaches and I have done powerful work aided by this book and the emotional intelligence test that comes with it. A fantastic combination for learning the skills that are critical to high job performance."

—Marshall Goldsmith, bestselling author of *What Got You Here Won't Get You There*, and premier executive educator as ranked by *The Wall Street Journal, Forbes, The Harvard Business Review,* and *Fast Company*

"At last a book that gives how to's rather than just what to's.

We need no more convincing that emotional intelligence is at the core of life success. What we need are practical ways of improving it. Bradberry and Greaves' brilliant new book is a godsend. It will change your life."

—Joseph Grenny, *New York Times* bestselling coauthor of *Crucial Conversations*

"This book is filled with wisdom, inspiration, and practical advice, rooted in groundbreaking research. The authors' positive strategies are immensely powerful and will change the way you look at your life, your work, and the world."

—Captain D. Michael Abrashoff, author of the bestseller *It's Your Ship*

"If you're wondering why your career is stalled or plateaued—or if you simply want to get on the fast track to the next level—this book is a must-read. Emotional intelligence is the sine qua non of success at work and this book gives you a quick-start to developing critical skills and behaviors to complement your technical expertise."

—Lois P. Frankel, Ph.D., *New York Times* bestselling author, *Nice Girls Don't Get the Corner Office*

"This book is a wake-up call for anyone who wants to dramatically improve their work life and strengthen their relationships. Drs. Bradberry and Greaves offer powerful research, practical strategies, and fascinating stories that will transform the way we think about ourselves and how we interact with those we care about the most."

—Jim Loehr, *New York Times* bestselling author,
The Power of Full Engagement

"I distributed the book to my entire team. We found it very helpful in our dealings with each other and our internal customers. With all the new buzzwords over the past few years, the heart and soul of a company's culture is how they support and promote emotional intelligence. Those with foresight see that emotional intelligence will separate the good companies from the great ones. This book is a wonderful tool for a grass-roots approach. If your desire is to be a truly resonant leader that people will trust and follow, this is an opportunity that cannot only change your professional career, but also your personal relationships."

—Regina Sacha, vice president, human resources,
FedEx Custom Critical

"In the fast lane of business life today, people spend more time on computer keyboards, BlackBerries and conference calls than they do in face-to-face communication. We're expected to piece together broken conversations, cryptic voicemails, and abbreviated text messages to figure out how to proceed. In this increasingly complex web, emotional intelligence is more important than ever before. This book is filled with invaluable insights and information that no one can afford to ignore."

—Rajeev Peshawaria, executive director,
Goldman Sachs International

"Drs. Bradberry and Greaves have created a gem that is powerful and easy to read. This book provides a captivating look at the things that matter most in life. Succeeding in Hollywood is as tough as any business, and emotional intelligence skills are essential. I highly recommend this book."

—Matt Olmstead, executive producer,
Prison Break and *NYPD Blue*

"This is a wonderful, practical, helpful book full of tools and techniques you can use to get along better with all the people in your life."

—Brian Tracy, bestselling author, *Eat That Frog*

"Drs. Bradberry and Greaves have succeeded in creating a practical summary of emotional intelligence. Without being simplistic, this book is accessible to managers and employees who need a quick yet sophisticated understanding of the topic. This book and TalentSmartEQ® e-learning are important components of Nokia's management and employee development programs."

—Jennifer Tsoulos, M.S., human resources, Nokia Mobile Phones

"Whip out your pen and get ready to take copious notes. This wonderful gem of a book is chock-a-block full of invaluable insights and incredibly useful suggestions—backed by strong scientific evidence. Word for word this is the most precious book I've read in a long time. I will give it to all my friends and clients as the one 'must read' for the season."

—Jim Belasco, *New York Times* bestselling coauthor, *Flight of the Buffalo*

"This book is a great resource for those of us charged with providing emergency services to the public. Through the simple and effective steps outlined in the book, I was able to learn and subsequently put into practice the emotional intelligence skills necessary to better relate to my customers during crisis situations. This book is a tool most supervisors should find useful in facilitating teamwork and promoting esprit de corps."

—Dominick Arena, fire captain, City of Escondido, California, Fire Department

"Emotional intelligence is a critical determinant of a physician's ultimate success or failure. Drs. Bradberry and Greaves have hit the bull's-eye with this timely research-based resource. I teach emotional intelligence in our faculty development leadership program, and I also mentor medical students. I can envision how this book can be woven into the medical school curriculum."

—Dixie Fisher, Ph.D., assistant professor of clinical, Keck School of Medicine, USC

"Success in my business is quantifiable and backing highly effective CEOs in our portfolio companies has been the key. There is no doubt in my mind that this book hits the nail on the head. Emotional intelligence in an individual determines the outcome more than any other factor, and is the one least understood. This book is a 'must read' for managers to gain insight and create a plan to improve their effectiveness as well as the success of the organization."

—Rick Hoskins, managing director, Genstar Capital, LLC

EMOTIONAL INTELLIGENCE 2.0

DR. TRAVIS BRADBERRY & DR. JEAN GREAVES

TalentSmartEQ

TalentSmartEQ

11526 Sorrento Valley Road
San Diego, CA 92121

**For information regarding special discounts for bulk purchases,
contact TalentSmartEQ® at:
888-818-SMART (toll free, US & Canada callers) or 858-509-0582**

Visit us online at www.TalentSmartEQ.com

For permission requests, please contact the publisher:
TalentSmart, Inc.
11526 Sorrento Valley Road San Diego, CA 92121
www.TalentSmartEQ.com.

*To the loyal TalentSmartEQ® certified
trainers and all who've attended their sessions.
Your passion is the breath of life for this book.*

CONTRIBUTORS

*The following individuals made significant
contributions to this book.*

Sue DeLazaro, M.S.

Melissa Monday, Ph.D.

Jean Riley, M.S.

Lac D. Su, M.S.

Nick Tasler, M.S.

Eric Thomas, M.B.A., M.S.

Evan Watkins, M.F.A.

Lindsey Zan, M.S.

CONTENTS

FOREWORD

Not education. Not experience. Not knowledge or intellectual horsepower. None of these serve as an adequate predictor as to why one person succeeds and another doesn't. There is something else going on that society doesn't seem to account for.

We see examples of this every day in our workplaces, our homes, our churches, our schools and our neighborhoods. We observe supposedly brilliant and well-educated people struggle, while others with fewer obvious skills or attributes flourish. And we ask ourselves why?

The answer almost always has to do with this concept called emotional intelligence. And while it is harder to identify and measure than IQ or experience, and certainly difficult to capture on a resume, its power cannot be denied.

And by now, it's not exactly a secret. People have been talking about emotional intelligence for a while, but somehow they haven't been able to harness its power. After all, as a society we continue to focus most of our self-improvement energy in the pursuit of knowledge, experience, intelligence and education. This would be fine if we could honestly say we had a full understanding of our emotions, not to mention the emotions of others, and an understanding of how our emotions influence our lives so fundamentally every day.

I think the reason for this gap between the popularity of emotional intelligence as a concept and its application in society is twofold. First, people just don't understand it. They often mistake emotional intelligence for a form of charisma or gregariousness. Second, they don't see it as something that can be improved. Either you have it or you don't.

And that's why this is such a helpful book. By understanding what emotional intelligence really is and how we can manage it in our lives, we can begin to leverage all of that intelligence, education and experience we've been storing up for all these years.

So, whether you've been wondering about emotional intelligence for years or know nothing about it, this book can drastically change the way you think about success. You might want to read it twice.

Patrick Lencioni
author of *The Five Dysfunctions of a Team*;
president of the Table Group

1

THE JOURNEY

The warm California sun greeted Butch Connor as he stepped out of his truck and onto the sands of Salmon Creek Beach. It was the first day of a long holiday weekend, and a perfect morning to grab his board and head out for a surf. Most of the other local surfers had the same idea that morning, and after 30 minutes or so, Butch decided to leave the crowd behind. He penetrated the water's surface with long, deep strokes that propelled him away from the pack and over to a stretch of beach where he could catch a few waves away from the crowd.

Once Butch had paddled a good 40 yards away from the other surfers, he sat up on his board and bobbed up and down in the rolling swells while he waited for a wave that caught his fancy. A beautiful teal wave began to crest as it approached the shoreline, and as Butch lay down on his board to catch the wave, a loud splash behind him stole his attention. Butch glanced over his right shoulder and froze in horror at the sight of a 14-inch, gray dorsal fin cutting through the water toward him. Butch's muscles locked up, and he lay there in a panic, gasping for air. He became hyper-focused on his surroundings; he could hear his heart pounding as he watched the sun glistening on the fin's moist surface.

The approaching wave stood tall to reveal Butch's worst nightmare in the shimmering, translucent surface—a massive great white shark that stretched 14 feet from nose to tail. Paralyzed by the fear coursing through his veins, Butch let the wave roll past, and with it a speedy ride to the safety of the shoreline. It was just the shark and him now; it swam in a semi-circle and approached him head-on. The shark drifted in slowly along his left side, and he was too transfixed by the proximity of the massive fish to notice his left leg dangling perilously off his surfboard in the frigid saltwater. *It's as big around as my Volkswagen*, Butch thought as the dorsal fin approached. He felt the sudden urge to reach out and touch the shark. *It's*

> **The approaching wave stood tall to reveal Butch's worst nightmare in the shimmering, translucent surface—a massive great white shark that stretched 14 feet from nose to tail.**

going to kill me anyway. Why shouldn't I touch it?

The shark didn't give him a chance. The shark, with a massive chomp of its jaws, thrust its head upward from underneath Butch's leg. Butch's leg stayed on top of the shark's rising, boulder-sized head and out of its cavernous mouth, and he fell off the opposite side of his surfboard into the murky water. Butch splashing into the water sent the shark into a spastic frenzy. The shark waved its head about maniacally while snapping its jaws open and shut. The great white struck nothing; it blasted water in all directions as it thrashed about. The irony of floating alongside a 3,000-pound killing machine without so much as a scratch was not lost on Butch. Neither was the grave reality that this apex predator was unlikely to miss again. Thoughts of escape and survival flooded Butch's mind as quickly and completely as terror had in the moments prior.

The shark stopped snapping and swam around Butch in tight circles. Instead of climbing back on his surfboard, Butch floated on his belly with his arms draped over the board. He rotated the surfboard as the shark circled, using the surfboard as a makeshift barrier between himself and the man-eater. Butch's fear morphed into anger as he waited for the beast to strike. The shark came at him again, and Butch decided it was time to put up a fight. He aimed the sharp, pointed nose of his surfboard at the shark as it approached. When it raised its head out of the water to bite, Butch jammed the nose of the board into the shark's slotted gills. This blow sent the shark into another bout of nervous thrashing. Butch climbed atop his board and yelled, "Shark!" at the pack of surfers down the beach. Butch's warning and the sight of the turbulent cauldron of whitewater around him sent the surfers racing for dry land.

Butch also paddled toward safety, but the shark stopped him dead in his tracks after just a few strokes. It surfaced in his path to the shoreline, and then began circling him once more. Butch came to the dire conclusion that his evasive tactics were merely delaying the inevitable, and a paralyzing fear took hold of him yet again. Butch lay there trembling on his surfboard while the shark circled. He mustered the will to keep the tip of his board pointed in the shark's direction, but he was too terror-stricken to get back in the water and use his board as a barrier.

Butch's thoughts raced between terror and sadness. He wondered what his three children were going to do without him and how long his girlfriend would take to move on with her life. He wanted to live. He wanted to escape this monster, and he needed to calm down if that was ever going to happen. Butch convinced himself that the shark could sense his fear like a rabid dog; he decided that he must get hold of himself because it was his fear that was motivating the shark to strike. To Butch's surprise, his body listened. The trembling subsided, and the blood returned to his arms and legs. He felt strong. He was ready to paddle. And paddle Butch did—straight for the shoreline. A healthy rip current ensured that his journey to shore was a nerve-rattling five minutes of paddling like mad with the sense that the shark was somewhere behind him and could strike at any moment. When Butch made it to the beach, an awestruck group of surfers and other beachgoers were waiting for him. The surfers thanked him profusely for the warning and patted him on the back. For Butch Connor, standing on dry land had never felt so good.

When Reason and Feeling Collide

Butch and the great white weren't fighting the only battle in the water that morning. Deep inside Butch's brain, his reason struggled for control of his behavior against an onslaught of intense emotions. The bulk of the time, his feelings won out, which was mostly to his detriment (paralyzing fear) but at times a benefit (the anger-fueled jab of his surfboard). With great effort, Butch was able to calm himself down, and—realizing the shark wasn't going away—make the risky paddle for shore that saved his life. Though most of us will never have to tussle with a great white shark, our brains battle it out like Butch's every single day.

The daily challenge of dealing effectively with emotions is critical to the human condition because our brains are hard-wired to give emotions the upper hand. Here's how it works: everything you see, smell, hear, taste and touch travels through your body in the form of electric signals. These signals pass from cell to cell until they reach their ultimate destination, your brain. They enter your brain at the base near the spinal cord, but must travel to your frontal lobe (behind your forehead) before reaching the place where rational, logical thinking takes place. The trouble is, they pass through your limbic system along the way—the place where emotions are produced. This journey ensures you experience things emotionally before your reason can kick into gear.

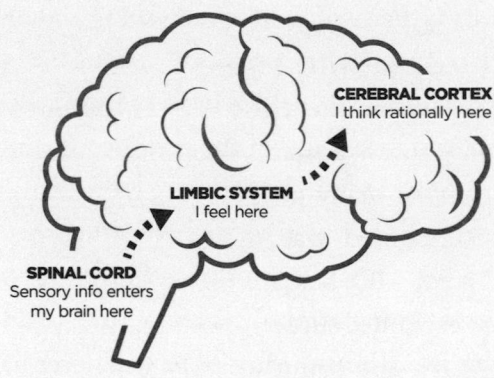

CEREBRAL CORTEX
I think rationally here

LIMBIC SYSTEM
I feel here

SPINAL CORD
Sensory info enters
my brain here

The physical pathway for emotional intelligence starts in the brain, at the spinal cord. Your primary senses enter here and must travel to the front of your brain before you can think rationally about your experience. But first they travel through the limbic system, the place where emotions are experienced. Emotional intelligence requires effective communication between the rational and emotional centers of the brain.

The rational area of your brain (the front of your brain) can't stop the emotion "felt" by your limbic system, but the two areas do influence each other and maintain constant communication. The communication between your emotional and rational "brains" is the physical source of emotional intelligence.

When emotional intelligence was first discovered, it served as the missing link in a peculiar finding: people with the highest levels of intelligence (IQ) outperform those with average IQs just 20 percent of the time, while people with average IQs outperform those with high IQs 70 percent of the time. This anomaly threw a massive wrench into what many people had always assumed was the source of success—IQ.

> **People with the highest levels of intelligence (IQ) outperform those with average IQs just 20% of the time, while people with average IQs outperform those with high IQs 70% of the time.**

Scientists realized there must be another variable that explained success above and beyond one's IQ, and years of research and countless studies pointed to emotional intelligence (EQ) as the critical factor.

A *Time* magazine cover and hours of television coverage introduced millions to EQ, and once people were exposed to it, they wanted to know more. They wanted to know how

EQ worked and who had it. Most importantly, people wanted to know if *they* had it. Books emerged to scratch this itch, including our own, *The Emotional Intelligence Quick Book*. Released in 2004, the Quick Book was unique because each copy contained a passcode that let the reader go online and take the world's most popular EQ test, the *Emotional Intelligence Appraisal®*. The book satisfied readers' curiosity by teaching the ins and outs of EQ and (thanks to the test) providing a new self-perspective that wasn't available anywhere else.

The Emotional Intelligence Quick Book hit home—it was an instant best seller that has been translated into 23 languages and is now available in more than 150 countries. But times have changed. The emotional intelligence field is on the steep incline of a new wave of understanding—how people can improve their EQ and make lasting gains that have a profoundly positive impact upon their lives. Just as knowing your EQ score was reserved for the privileged few before the publication of *The Emotional Intelligence Quick Book*, learning how to increase your EQ is something that happens only in isolated circles. Our company trains hundreds of people each week to increase their EQ, but even at this pace it would take 3,840 years to hit every adult currently residing in the U.S.! We realize that we've unwittingly been holding important information back. We believe everyone should have the opportunity to increase his or her EQ, and have created this book to make it possible.

Your Journey

Emotional Intelligence 2.0 has one purpose—increasing your EQ. These pages will take you far beyond knowing what EQ is and how you score. You'll discover time-tested strategies that you can begin using today to take your EQ to new heights. As you transform yourself and bring new skills into your life, you'll reap all of the benefits that this incredible human ability has to offer.

The 66 strategies in this book are the result of many years of careful testing with people just like you. These strategies provide the specifics of what you need to say, do, and think to increase your EQ. To glean everything they have to offer, you need to know where to focus your attention. The first major step in your journey to a higher EQ is to go online and take the *Emotional Intelligence Appraisal®* test. Taking the test now provides a baseline against which you can gauge your improvement as you read on and learn. Measuring your EQ takes your learning beyond a conceptual or motivational exercise—your score profile uncovers the EQ skills you need to improve the most, and it pinpoints the individual strategies from this book that will get you there. This feature takes the guesswork out of choosing the strategies that will increase your EQ the most.

The value of measuring your EQ now is akin to learning the waltz with an actual partner. If I tell you how the dance works, you are likely to learn something and may even get the urge to try it yourself. If, as I show you how to do a waltz, you practice each step with a partner, your chances of remembering them later on the dance floor go up exponentially. The EQ profile you receive from taking the *Emotional Intelligence Appraisal®* is your dance partner in developing these skills. It will remind you where to step with every beat of the music.

Your online report includes a development plan that summarizes the skills you are working on and provides automatic reminders to help you stay focused. You will also learn the next steps to take to practice high EQ strategies.

In addition to receiving the most accurate scores possible, taking the *Emotional Intelligence Appraisal®* now lets you see how much your EQ scores increase with time. You can take the test twice—once now and again after you've had enough time to practice and adopt the strategies from this book. After you complete the test a second time, your updated feedback report will display your scores side by side and offer insights into how you've changed and what your next steps should be to keep your EQ working for you. The orange insert at the back of this book contains instructions for going online to access the *Emotional Intelligence Appraisal®*, as well as the unique passcode that you'll need to access the test.

Emotions can help you and they can hurt you, but you have no say in the matter until you understand them. We invite you to begin your journey now, because we know that emotional mastery and understanding can become realities for you.

2

___

THE BIG PICTURE

Before you take a closer look at each of the four EQ skills in the next chapter, there are some important things you need to know about EQ as a whole. Since 2002, we've tested millions of people to explore the role emotions play in daily living. We've learned how people see themselves versus what others see, and we've observed how various choices affect personal and professional success.

Despite the growing focus on EQ, a global deficit in understanding and managing emotions remains. Only 36 percent of the people we tested are able to accurately identify their emotions as they happen. This means that two thirds of us are typically

> **Only 36 percent of the people we tested are able to accurately identify their emotions as they happen.**

controlled by our emotions and are not yet skilled at spotting them and using them to our benefit. Emotional awareness and understanding are not taught in school. We enter the workforce knowing how to read, write, and report on bodies of knowledge, but too often, we lack the skills to manage our emotions in the heat of the challenging problems that we face. Good decisions require far more than factual knowledge. They are made using self-knowledge and emotional mastery when they're needed most.

Considering the range of emotions people express, it's no wonder they can get the better of us. We have so many words to describe the feelings that surface in life, yet all emotions are derivations of five core feelings: happiness, sadness, anger, fear, and shame. As you move through your daily routine—whether you're working, spending time with family or friends, eating, exercising, relaxing, or even sleeping—you are subject to a constant stream of emotions. It is so easy to forget that we have emotional reactions to almost everything that happens in our lives, whether we notice them or not. The complexity of these emotions is revealed in their varying forms of intensity.

INTENSITY OF FEELINGS	HAPPY	SAD	ANGRY	AFRAID	ASHAMED
HIGH	Elated Excited Overjoyed Thrilled Exuberant Ecstatic Fired up Passionate	Depressed Agonized Alone Hurt Dejected Hopeless Sorrowful Miserable	Furious Enraged Outraged Boiling Irate Seething Loathsome Betrayed	Terrified Horrified Scared stiff Petrified Fearful Panicky Frantic Shocked	Sorrowful Remorseful Defamed Worthless Disgraced Dishonored Mortified Admonished
MEDIUM	Cheerful Gratified Good Relived Satisfied Glowing	Heartbroken Somber Lost Distressed Let down Melancholy	Upset Mad Defended Frustrated Agitated Disgusted	Apprehensive Frightened Threatened Insecure Uneasy Intimidated	Apologetic Unworthy Sneaky Guilty Embarrassed Secretive
LOW	Glad Contented Pleasant Tender Pleased Mellow	Unhappy Moody Blue Upset Disappointed Dissatisfied	Perturbed Annoyed Uptight Resistant Irritated Touchy	Cautious Nervous Worried Timid Unsure Anxious	Bashful Ridiculous Regretful Uncomfortable Pitied Silly

The five core emotions run left to right across the top of the table. Manifestations of each emotion based upon the intensity felt are described down each of the columns in the table. Adapted from and reproduced by permission from Julia West.

Triggers and Emotional Hijackings

While Butch Connor was being attacked by a great white shark, he experienced several emotional hijackings—moments when his emotions controlled his behavior and he reacted without thinking. Typically, the more intense your emotions are, the greater the likelihood that they will dictate your actions. Matters of life or death—such as being attacked by a massive beast—are certain to induce a temporary emotional hijacking.

In Butch's case, emotional hijackings left him paralyzed by fear, but even in the presence of a man-eater, Butch was able to use his thoughts to take back control from his emotions. Butch reasoned with himself until the paralysis subsided and he was calm enough to complete the paddle to shore. Butch's thoughts didn't make his feelings of fear and terror disappear, but they *did* keep his emotions from hijacking his behavior.

Since our brains are wired to make us emotional creatures, your first reaction to an event is always going to be an emotional one. You have no control over this part of the process. You *do* control the thoughts that follow an emotion, and you have a great deal of say in how you react to an emotion—as long as you are aware of it. Some experiences produce emotions that you are easily aware of; other times, emotions may seem nonexistent. When something generates a prolonged emotional reaction in you, it's called a "trigger event." Your reaction to your triggers is shaped by your personal history, which includes your experience with similar situations. As your EQ skills grow, you'll learn to spot your triggers and practice productive ways of responding that will become habitual.

Sizing Up the Whole Person

Emotional intelligence is your ability to recognize and understand emotions in yourself and others, and your ability to use this awareness to manage your behavior and relationships. Emotional intelligence is the "something" in each of us that is a bit intangible. It affects how we manage behavior, navigate social complexities, and make personal decisions that achieve positive results.

Emotional intelligence taps into a fundamental element of human behavior that is distinct from your intellect. There is no known connection between IQ and EQ; you simply can't predict EQ based on how smart someone is. Cognitive intelligence, or IQ, is not flexible. Your IQ, short of a traumatic event such as a brain injury, is fixed from birth. You don't get smarter by learning new facts or information. Intelligence is your *ability* to learn, and it's the same at age 15 as it is at age 50. EQ, on the other hand, is a flexible skill that can be learned. While it is true that some people are naturally more emotionally intelligent than others, a high EQ can be developed even if you aren't born with it.

Personality is the final piece in the puzzle. It's the stable "style" that defines each of us. Your personality is a result of your preferences, such as your inclination to introversion or extroversion. However, like IQ, personality can't be used to predict emotional intelligence. Also like IQ, personality is stable over a lifetime. Personality traits appear early in life, and they don't go away. People often assume that certain traits (for

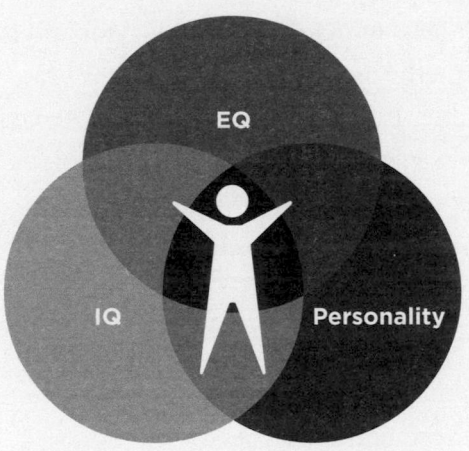

IQ, personality, and EQ are distinct qualities we all possess. Together, they determine how we think and act. It is impossible to predict one based upon another. People may be intelligent but not emotionally intelligent, and people of all types of personalities can be high in EQ and/or IQ. Of the three, EQ is the only quality that is flexible and able to change.

example, extroversion) are associated with a higher EQ, but those who prefer to be with other people are no more emotionally intelligent than people who prefer to be alone. You can use your personality to assist in developing your EQ, but the latter isn't dependent on the former. EQ is a flexible skill, while personality does not change. Assessing IQ, EQ, and personality together is the best way to get a picture of the whole person. When you measure all three in a single individual, they don't overlap much. Instead, each covers unique ground that helps to explain what makes a person tick.

The Impact of EQ

How much of an impact does EQ have on your professional success? The short answer is: *a lot!* It's a powerful way to focus your energy in one direction with a tremendous result. We've tested EQ alongside 33 other important skills and found that it subsumes the majority of them, including time management, decision-making, and communication. Your EQ is the foundation for a host of critical skills—it impacts most everything you say and do each day.

> **EQ is so critical to success that it accounts for 58 percent of performance in all types of jobs.**

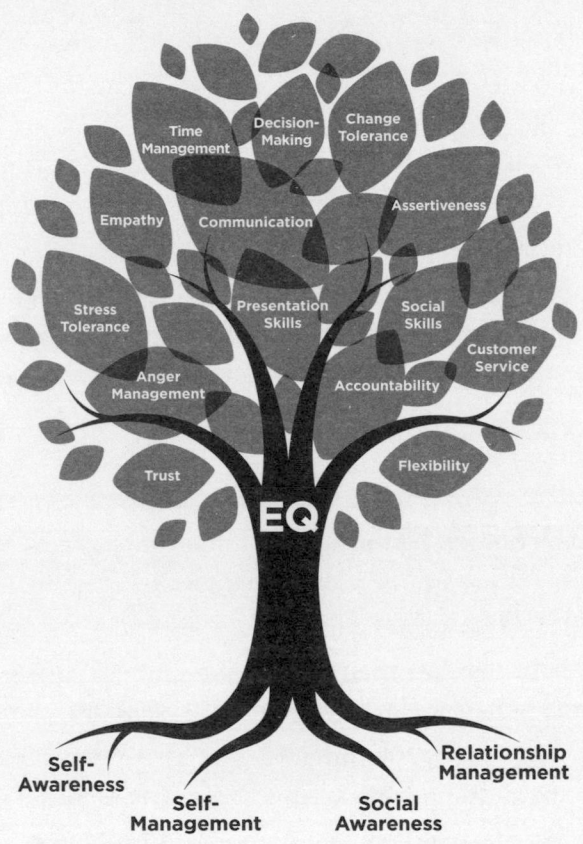

EQ is the foundation for a host of critical skills. A little effort spent on increasing your EQ tends to have a wide-ranging, positive impact on your life.

EQ is so critical to success that it accounts for 58 percent of performance in all types of jobs. It's the single biggest predictor of performance in the workplace and the strongest driver of leadership and personal excellence.

No matter whether people measure high or low in EQ, they can work to improve it, and those who score low can actually catch up to their coworkers. Research conducted at the business school at the University of Queensland in Australia discovered that people who are low in EQ and job performance can match their colleagues who excel in both—solely by working to improve their EQ.

Of all the people we've studied at work, we have found that 90 percent of high performers are also high in EQ. On the flip side, just 20 percent of low performers are high in EQ. You can be a high performer without EQ, but the chances are slim. People who develop their EQ tend to be successful on the job because the two go hand in hand. Naturally, people with high EQs make more money—an average of $29,000 more per year than people with low EQs. The link between EQ and earnings is so direct that every point increase in EQ adds $1,300 to an annual salary. These findings hold true for people in all

> **The link between EQ and earnings is so direct that every point increase in EQ adds $1,300 to an annual salary.**

industries, at all levels, in every region of the world. We haven't yet been able to find a job in which performance and pay aren't tied closely to EQ.

In order to be successful and fulfilled nowadays, you must learn to maximize your EQ skills, for those who employ a unique blend of reason and feeling achieve the greatest results. The remainder of this book will show you how to make this happen.

3

WHAT EMOTIONAL INTELLIGENCE LOOKS LIKE: UNDERSTANDING THE FOUR SKILLS

To truly improve your ability in the four emotional intelligence skills, you need to better understand each skill and what it looks like in action. The four emotional intelligence skills pair up under two primary competencies: personal competence and social competence. Personal competence is made up of your self-awareness and self-management skills, which focus

> **To truly improve your ability in the four emotional intelligence skills, you need to better understand each skill and what it looks like in action.**

more on you individually than on your interactions with other people. Personal competence is your ability to stay aware of your emotions and manage your behavior and tendencies.

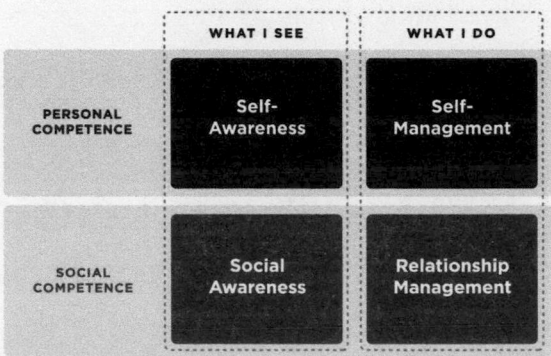

The four skills that together make up emotional intelligence. The top two skills, self-awareness and self-management, are more about you. The bottom two skills, social awareness and relationship management, are more about how you are with other people.

Social competence is made up of your social awareness and relationship management skills; social competence is your ability to understand other people's moods, behavior and motives in order to improve the quality of your relationships.

Self-Awareness

Self-awareness is your ability to accurately perceive your own emotions in the moment and understand your tendencies across situations. Self-awareness includes staying on top of your typical reactions to specific events, challenges, and people. A keen understanding of your tendencies is important; it helps you quickly make sense of your emotions. A high degree of self-awareness requires a willingness to tolerate the discomfort of focusing on feelings that may be negative.

The only way to genuinely understand your emotions is to spend enough time thinking through them to figure out where they come from and why they are there. Emotions always serve a purpose. Because they are your reactions to the world around you, emotions always come from somewhere. Many times emotions seem to arise out of thin air, and it's important to understand why something gets a reaction out of you. People who do this can cut to the core of a feeling quickly. Situations that create strong emotions will always require more thought, and these prolonged periods of self-reflection often keep you from doing something that you'll regret.

Self-awareness is not about discovering deep, dark secrets or unconscious motivations, but, rather, it comes from developing a straightforward and honest understanding of what makes you tick. People high in self-awareness are remarkably clear in their understanding of what they do well, what motivates and satisfies them, and which people and situations push their buttons.

The surprising thing about self-awareness is that just

thinking about it helps you improve the skill, even though much of your focus initially tends to be on what you do "wrong." Having self-awareness means you aren't afraid of your emotional "mistakes." They tell you what you should be doing differently and provide the steady stream of information you need to understand as your life unfolds.

Self-awareness is a foundational skill; when you have it, self-awareness makes the other emotional intelligence skills much easier to use. As self-awareness increases, people's satisfaction with life—defined as their ability to reach their goals at work and at home—skyrockets. Self-awareness is so important for job performance that 83 percent of people high in self-awareness are top performers, and just 2 percent of bottom performers are high in self-awareness. Why is this so? When you are self-aware you are far more likely to pursue the right opportunities, put your strengths to work and—perhaps most importantly—keep your emotions from holding you back.

The need for self-awareness has never been greater. Guided by the mistaken notion that psychology deals exclusively with pathology, we assume that the only time to learn about ourselves is in the face of crisis. We tend to embrace those things with which we're comfortable, and put the blinders on the moment something makes us uncomfortable. But it's really the whole picture that serves us. The more we understand the beauty and the blemishes, the better we are able to achieve our full potential.

What Self-Awareness Looks Like

**Dave T., regional service manager
Self-awareness score = 95***

What people who work with him say:

"Dave has clear long-term goals, and he doesn't make sacrifices for short-term gains. Dave is an 'up-front' kind of guy who doesn't play 'mind games' with people. I have witnessed this at company meetings and in meetings with customers."

"The best example I can provide for Dave is his move to our company. I'm sure there was an intense desire to make changes within the local team right out of the gate, but Dave took extra care to diagnose the situation, the team, and the customer prior to offering suggestions or mandates for change."

"In short, Dave manages his emotions; they don't manage him. I've seen him accept difficult business news with a brief frown, and then he quickly moves beyond that and partners with his team to find solutions to improve the situation."

*Scores are on the 1 to 100-point scale from the *Emotional Intelligence Appraisal®*. Scores and coworker comments are from actual people, though names and other identifying information have been altered.

Maria M., human resources manager
Self-awareness score = 90

What people who work with her say:

"In every situation that I have been involved with, good or bad, Maria has always remained calm, cool, and collected—even at times when I know she must have felt frustrated or angry. Maria is really honest about what she is feeling without getting bent out of shape about it. When faced with a difficult situation, she knows how to be firm and still kind at the same time."

"She is open and authentic at all times, and it is so meaningful to everyone that she interacts with. I would suggest that Maria not change: however, she can get a bit tougher sooner in some cases. She is aware of this and watches to ensure that she does not let kindness get in the way."

"During challenging situations with employees, Maria is very aware of her tone and makes an effort to keep the conversation appropriate. People here trust her."

What a Lack of Self-Awareness Looks Like

Tina J., marketing manager
Self-awareness score = 69

What people who work with her say:

"On occasion, Tina's stress and sense of urgency are projected/pushed on to other people. It would be good for her to better understand how her behavior affects others' work and emotional stress. Also, she sometimes comes across as defensive or aggressive, so for her to be more aware of her tone and language would be helpful."

"When things are going well for Tina, her emotional intelligence skills are stronger. She needs to learn to read herself and recognize her triggers so that she can respond more effectively when triggered."

"She needs to become aware of how she is perceived. She can come across as being very demanding, but I don't believe she means to."

Giles B., operations director
Self-awareness score = 67

What people who work with him say:

"Giles is very much in his 'own little world.' He obviously does care about his coworkers, but he doesn't seem to know where to draw a line. His personality can be overwhelming, but he doesn't notice when the other person is feeling annoyed, frustrated, or overwhelmed by him."

"When working with customers, he is very good at talking about the products and services we offer. On group projects, sometimes he gets so focused on the outcome, the process is missed. If he were to take a moment and let all the emotions settle, then take a look at the options to reach the desired outcome, things would go more smoothly."

"Giles is passionate about what he does. Sometimes that passion gets in the way. He might not notice that I am busy with something else before he jumps in and starts talking to me. When he is excited, he talks over you, and it is hard to get a word in edgewise. He doesn't mean to; he just is excited about what he does."

Self-Management

Self-management is what happens when you act—or do not act. It is dependent on your self-awareness and is the second major part of personal competence. Self-management is your ability to use your awareness of your emotions to stay flexible and direct your behavior positively. This means managing your emotional reactions to situations and people. Some emotions create a paralyzing fear that makes your thinking so cloudy that the best course of action is nowhere to be found—assuming that there is something you should be doing. In these cases, self-management is revealed by your ability to tolerate the uncertainty as you explore your emotions and options. Once you understand and build comfort with what you are feeling, the best course of action will show itself.

Self-management is more than resisting explosive or problematic behavior. The biggest challenge that people face is managing their tendencies over time and applying their skills in a variety of situations. Obvious and momentary opportunities for self-control (i.e., "I'm so mad at that darn dog!") are the easiest to spot and manage. Real results come from putting your momentary needs on

> **Real results come from putting your momentary needs on hold to pursue larger, more important goals.**

hold to pursue larger, more important goals. The realization of such goals is often delayed, meaning that your commitment to self-management will be tested over and over again. Those who manage themselves the best are able to see things through without cracking. Success comes to those who can put their needs on hold and continually manage their tendencies.

What Self-Management Looks Like

**Lane L., healthcare administrator
Self-management score = 93**

What people who work with her say:

"Lane is the epitome of patience and understanding during heated, emotionally-charged meetings. Others around her become fully embroiled in the discussions, and Lane actively listens and responds with knowledge and wisdom."

"I have seen first-hand how well she deals with difficult situations (i.e., termination of an employee). Lane is sensitive, yet direct and to the point. She listens patiently and sets a high standard of conduct."

"Lane is great one-on-one. She communicates well and thinks on her feet. Her reaction to crisis is excellent. Her ability to separate emotion from logic makes her a good tactical manager. I wish there were many more of her."

Yeshe M., computer programmer
Self-management score = 91

What people who work with him say:

"Yeshe handles stressful and confrontational situations very well. No matter how harshly project managers (PMs) hammer Yeshe, he never loses his cool! This gives him a lot of credibility with the PMs. He's also able to work with other people whose working style he isn't a fan of. I know going back and forth with them can be frustrating sometimes, but Yeshe never loses his patience."

"I've seen Yeshe in an extremely frustrating situation where he couldn't get something done because other people didn't do their jobs. He dealt with it politely and professionally. He was able to explain the procedure again in order to achieve the best possible solution, even though he was upset."

"I have never heard Yeshe speak negatively about someone who has a different opinion or idea. A lot of talking behind people's backs happens around here, and he doesn't give into the temptation, even when he feels strongly about an issue."

What a Lack of Self-Management Looks Like

**Jason L., information technology consultant
Self-management score = 59**

What people who work with him say:

"In stressful situations, or when something goes wrong, Jason sometimes responds too quickly, sharply, or disjointedly. I wish Jason would take some time to cool off and slow down before responding. He's so emotional. I have seen his coworkers respond in disbelief to the manner in which he communicated with them. Jason means well but can panic when he is stressed. His reactions trickle onto his teammates."

"Jason should be more aware of his verbal outbursts, and how they affect both clients and coworkers. He is not mean-spirited; he cares a great deal about others but these verbal miscues are just that—outbursts that need to be thought out before expressed. These happen more when he is stressed . . . as the old commercial says, he shouldn't let them see him sweat so much."

"Jason lets his emotions rule his behavior. Sometimes he acts or speaks hurriedly. I wish he would be a bit more patient and give the situation an opportunity to work itself out before reacting. Many times these situations resolve themselves or aren't quite as urgent as he perceives, but before you know it, he's heightened the intensity with a flurry of messages."

Mei S., regional sales director
Self-management score = 61

What people who work with her say:

"Mei needs to not be so honest. Her staff don't need to know about all of the bull that goes down at corporate. If certain things upset her, she needs to learn to keep them to herself. When she is unhappy, it sets the tone for our team. Mei tends to radiate stress in certain situations, and as a leader, it impacts her team negatively by creating stress and negativity rather than diffusing them."

"Mei has a hard time congratulating staff for their accomplishments, and it comes across as jealousy. It feels like I am in competition with her rather than feeling like she wants me to succeed. I think Mei is a great sales professional, and she treats clients well. I wish she would give her employees the same treatment."

"Mei needs to be proactive instead of reactive. In times of crisis, she shouldn't reveal to everyone how stressed she is. She's so focused and driven to personally succeed that perhaps she takes on too much herself. She has a demanding workload managing the West Coast Team, but she needs to hold her emotions back when people vent about their own problems in meetings."

Social Awareness

As the first component of social competence, social awareness is a foundational skill. Social awareness is your ability to accurately pick up on emotions in other people and understand what is really going on with them. This often means perceiving what other people are thinking and feeling even if you do not feel the same way. It's easy to get caught up in your own emotions and forget to consider the perspective of the other party. Social awareness ensures you stay focused and absorb critical information.

Listening and observing are the most important elements of social awareness. To listen well and observe what's going on around us, we have to stop doing many things we like to do. We have to stop talking, stop the monologue that may be running through our minds, stop anticipating the point the other person is about to make, and stop thinking ahead to what we are going to say next. It takes practice to really watch people as you interact with them and get a good sense of what they are thinking and feeling. At times, you'll feel like an anthropologist. Anthropologists make their living watching others in their natural state without letting their own thoughts and feelings disturb the observation. This is social awareness in its purest form. The difference is you won't be 100 yards away watching events unfold through a pair of binoculars. To be socially aware, you have to spot and understand people's emotions while you're right there in the middle of it—a contributing, yet astutely aware, member of the interaction.

What Social Awareness Looks Like

| **Alfonso J., pharmaceutical sales manager**
| **Social awareness score = 96**

What people who work with him say:

"Alfonso has a rare talent to be able to read the emotions of others very well. He adjusts to different situations and manages to build relationships with almost anyone. Good examples are dinners, meetings, and ride-alongs with reps."

"Alfonso does an excellent job relating to the frustrations reps have with other departments within our company. He is always looking out for his reps, and has the ability to put himself in the reps' shoes, and ask himself what is wrong with the situation. People become very loyal to Alfonso."

"Alfonso recognizes emotions very effectively when it comes to the end-of-month numbers and end-of-year numbers with his reps, getting the most out of his team. He was great at building relationships with the surgeons at the dinner table because he could read how to lead the conversation without them feeling like they were being controlled."

Maya S., organizational development executive
Social awareness score = 92

What people who work with her say:

"Maya has an uncanny ability to spot and address the elephant in the room. She does a good job acknowledging other people's feelings when communicating difficult news. She reflects how others are feeling, and adapts her communication style to help reach a resolution. She gets to know people on a personal level so she can better understand their perspectives and work well with them."

"Maya is great in executive team meetings where she respectfully listens to her peers and then offers her opinion. She has a sincere interest in understanding people and offers them valuable insights based on what they're saying or doing. She is a good team-builder who strengthens bonds within the team."

"Maya is the most effective 'active listener' I have ever seen. She is skilled at communicating the 'context' for her comments with the goal of ensuring understanding. She is respectful toward others while being able to establish her authority. Maya motivates and inspires people. She can uplift people and put them at ease."

What a Lack of Social Awareness Looks Like

Craig C., attorney
Social awareness score = 55

What people who work with him say:

"Craig needs to allow others to feel good about their ideas, even when he has a better plan. He also needs to be more patient, and allow them to have equally effective plans that are just different from his plan. I would like him to seek to understand what people are feeling and thinking and notice what evidence there is regarding situations before speaking his opinion or offering solutions."

"Craig needs to listen better. He needs to pay attention to what is being said rather than thinking about what he wants to say. It is usually apparent in his body language that he is not listening, which puts people off. I also wish that he would be more accurate when representing other people's ideas."

"Craig is not one to socialize. He is so focused on work and sometimes comes across as not interested in what's going on with a person on that particular day. When he has new ideas (or ideas from his former firm), he has a hard time explaining them so the staff will accept them. Craig should learn to listen to others with his ears and with his heart. He seems to have a 'hardening of his positions,' and it makes him unwilling to accept other people's viewpoints or include their input in his decisions."

Rachel M., project manager
Social awareness score = 62

What people who work with her say:

"Rachel misses the non-technical currents in meetings. The mood and evolution of opinions are lost on her. Rachel needs to learn to absorb the non-technical, human side of meetings and become a student of people and their feelings."

"Rachel gets singularly focused on a particular issue and does not see the forest for the trees. This can get frustrating for those of us around her. She is typically oblivious to our reactions. She should check with everyone around the table to calibrate where their head is at before getting too enmeshed in the details of her project. She would be better served by framing the topic in large chunks rather than taking everyone through the details straight away."

"Rachel can sometimes get so caught up in her own thoughts during meetings and one-on-one conversations that she is not really listening to either the explicit or implicit dialogue going on. This makes her less effective because she is not actively participating in the ongoing conversation and misses opportunities to influence the direction. Rachel needs to work on considering issues from the other person's agenda or point of view so that she can more effectively influence, or at least directly address, their perspective. It will also help her to work on making her conversations as concise and targeted as possible. People can lose interest or get confused during long explanations, or when they are unclear about the message."

Relationship Management

Though relationship management is the second component of social competence, this skill often taps into your abilities in the first three emotional intelligence skills: self-awareness, self-management, and social awareness. Relationship management is your ability to use your awareness of your own emotions and those of others to manage interactions successfully. This ensures clear communication and effective handling of conflict. Relationship management is also the bond you build with others over time. People who manage relationships well are able to see the benefit of connecting with many different people, even those they are not fond of. Solid relationships are something that should be sought and cherished. They are the result of how you understand people, how you treat them, and the history you share.

The weaker the connection you have with someone, the harder it is to get your point across. If you want people to listen, you have to practice relationship management and seek benefits from every relationship, especially the challenging ones. The difference between an interaction and a relationship is a matter of frequency. It's a product of the quality, depth, and time you spend interacting with another person.

Relationship management poses the greatest challenge for most people during times of stress. When you consider that more than 70 percent of the people we've tested have difficulty handling stress, it's easy to see why building quality relationships poses a challenge. Some of the most challenging and stressful situations people face are at work. Conflicts at work tend to fester when people passively avoid problems, because people lack the skills needed to initiate a direct, yet constructive conversation. Conflicts at work tend to explode when people don't manage their anger or frustration, and choose to take it out on other people. Relationship management gives you the skills you need to avoid both scenarios, and make the most out of every interaction you have with another person.

What Relationship Management Looks Like

Gail C., chief financial officer
Relationship management score = 95

What people who work with her say:

"Gail has an innate ability to read people and their emotions, and she uses what she learns to create a safe and inviting forum for discussion. There has never been a time that Gail's door was not 'open' when I have needed her, and she always manages to maintain a pleasant and professional manner even when her workload is demanding. People know that they can count on Gail and what they say to her in confidence will be respected and not repeated."

"Gail is very sensitive to others and tries to make situations better. When someone is upset, she asks just enough questions to get a handle on the situation, and then is able to give concrete advice and help to the person, making them feel 100% better. Gail makes you feel smart and confident when she delivers feedback, even if you've made a mistake. She helps her staff improve and grow, and she sets a good example for dealing with people assertively and speaking up."

"Even during tough conversations, Gail is concerned about

maintaining good, comfortable relationships with all parties involved. Gail finds out something about the other person's interests and inquires about it when meeting, even if it appears there is no common ground. Gail has a firm handle on her own emotions and almost seems to feel what you feel when she is talking with you, which helps you feel like she relates to you and understands you."

Allister B., physician
Relationship management score = 93

What people who work with him say:

"Allister is a wonderfully patient, empathetic listener, which is why his patients love him. He tries very hard to be nonjudgmental and gives people the benefit of the doubt. He is the same way with the nurses and technicians. I've seen Allister in situations where his patients' families were asking difficult questions, and he was able to remain calm and answer without alienating the family member asking the questions. He listens carefully to what others say and never shows if he is upset or bothered by it. He responds kindly but with authority."

"Allister's interaction skills are supreme. In situations that I've witnessed him less than pleased with a specific outcome, he has always expressed his position with thoughtful insight about his expectations without anger or outburst. I'd describe him as direct, yet free from confrontation or sounding out of control. He is also quick to praise the staff 's efforts and success when deserving. He is good at seeing the overall picture and then counseling in a compassionate and realistic manner."

"I have never left Allister feeling anything less than 110%. He knows when to approach an issue sensitively, and knows when to give praise and encouragement. Allister knows his colleagues very well, and this enables him to handle conflict in a calm and positive manner. He's respected for collecting feedback before drawing conclusions. He tries to find the best way to communicate with others, even when there's an atmosphere of resistance, confusion, or outright conflict. His ability to empathize with others is outstanding, and It creates positive, strong relationships."

What a Lack of Relationship Management Looks Like

Dave M., sales manager
Relationship management score = 66

What people who work with him say:

"If Dave doesn't see eye-to-eye with someone, he makes it apparent that it's not worth developing the relationship. I wish that he would still dedicate the time and resources necessary to make a win for the territory. When he feels that a certain person he is working with may not be an 'ally' but someone not to be trusted, he will be very clear about his opinion about that person. This has a ripple effect on the people he tells, and it erodes camaraderie. Dave is usually effective when he gets to know people better, and trusts that they are not a threat, but he'll have to get over this if he wants to keep climbing the ladder."

"Dave can get over-excited when meeting new people and this can be a good trait, but some people don't respond to his enthusiasm, and they pull back from him. It makes it hard for them to connect with him. I would like to see Dave work on unifying his team, and dispel the feeling that some decisions are made based on his personal opinion or bias. Too often, people feel as if they've had their professional opinion ignored in spite of providing a solid foundation for that opinion."

"Dave always reacts to people rather than responding to them. To have a strong opinion is fine, but to dismiss others' thoughts is not. He also needs to tailor his communication style to the person. His approach is nearly always very direct, which can be difficult for some people to handle."

Natalie T., floor supervisor
Relationship management score = 69

What people who work with her say:

"Natalie often minimizes a person's point of view or experience. She justifies bad situations by stating that it could always be worse, you just don't understand, or you should just get over it. She comes across as blunt and not empathetic, particularly with her subordinates. I want her to be more genuine in her interactions with them, and show a general appreciation for others."

"Natalie needs to stop finding faults in every situation. It is tiring and demotivating. She needs to start recognizing people's achievements. There is a stigma that exists that Natalie is tough, difficult to work for, and unapproachable. She may achieve results, but at the expense of others."

"I would like to see Natalie avoid making judgmental or negative statements to her team, or others, when her statements add no value. Helping people see what could be done different helps them develop, but her continued negative feedback comes across as her feeling the need to belittle people. People no longer value her input, and at times view it as her need to be seen as superior."

4

—

DIGGING IN: MY EMOTIONAL INTELLIGENCE ACTION PLAN

Information travels between the rational and emotional centers of your brain much as cars do on a city street. When you practice EQ skills, the traffic flows smoothly in both directions. Increases in the traffic strengthen the connection between the rational and emotional centers of your brain. Your EQ is greatly affected by your ability to keep this road well traveled. The more you think about what you are feeling—and do something productive with that feeling—the more developed this pathway becomes. Some of us struggle along a two-lane country road, while others have built a five-lane superhighway. Whether the former or the latter best describes you, there's always room to add lanes. "Plasticity" is the term neurologists use to describe the brain's ability to change. Your brain grows new connections much as your biceps might swell if you started curling heavy weights several times a week. The change is gradual, and the weight becomes easier and easier to lift the longer you stick to your routine. Your brain can't swell like your biceps since it's confined by your skull, so instead the brain cells develop new connections to speed the efficiency of thought without increasing its size.

As you apply the strategies from the remaining chapters to increase your EQ skills, the billions of microscopic neurons lining the road between the rational and emotional centers of your brain will branch off small "arms" (much like a tree branch) to reach out to the other cells. A single cell can grow 15,000 connections with its neighbors. This chain reaction of growth ensures the pathway of thought responsible for the behavior grows strong, making it easier to kick this new resource into action in the future.

> **A single cell can grow 15,000 connections with its neighbors. This chain reaction of growth ensures the pathway of thought responsible for the behavior grows strong, making it easier to kick this new resource into action in the future.**

You'll have to practice the strategies repeatedly before they'll become your own. It can require tremendous effort to get a new behavior going, but once you train your brain it becomes a habit. If you typically yell when you are feeling angry, for example, you have to learn to choose an alternative reaction. You must practice this new reaction many times before it will replace the urge to yell. In the beginning, doing something other than yelling when you are angry will be extremely difficult. But each time you succeed, the new pathway is strengthened. Eventually the urge to yell is so small that it's easy to ignore. Studies have demonstrated a lasting change in EQ more than six years after new skills were first adopted.

The Emotional Intelligence Action Plan that follows will help you to focus your efforts more effectively as you explore and apply the EQ strategies in the remaining chapters. Follow these steps to complete your Emotional Intelligence Action Plan:

1. **Transfer your *Emotional Intelligence Appraisal*® scores onto part one (My Journey Begins) of your Emotional Intelligence Action Plan on page 56.** Go ahead and write right on the pages of this book.

2. **Pick an EQ skill to work on.** The human mind can focus effectively on one EQ skill at a time. Even the most ambitious people should trust that working diligently on a single

skill will take you far—your ability in other EQ skills will piggyback on your efforts. Your feedback report from the Emotional Intelligence Appraisal ® test recommends a skill for you to start with. You may choose a skill on your own instead, but we recommend you don't start with relationship management if you scored lower than 75 in all four EQ skills.

3. **Pick three strategies to begin using for your chosen skill.** Your feedback report from the *Emotional Intelligence Appraisal*® recommends specific strategies from this book based on an analysis of your score profile. Feel free to choose from these recommendations, or choose different strategies from the strategies chapter for your chosen skill.

4. **Choose an EQ mentor.** Find someone who is gifted in your chosen EQ skill, and ask this person if he or she is willing to offer you feedback and guidance at regular intervals during your journey. Be certain to set up a regular meeting time, and write this person's name in your action plan.

5. **Keep the following in mind as you apply your chosen strategies:**
   a. **Expect success, not perfection.** When it comes to developing new EQ skills, perfection means you aren't pushing yourself hard enough. You'll need to continue

to catch yourself when your emotions get the best of you, if you want to keep improving.

b. **Practice, practice, practice.** Sheer quantity of practice is the real secret to increasing your EQ skills. Practice your EQ strategies as often as you can, in a variety of situations, and with all types of people.

c. **Be patient.** When you work to improve your EQ, it will take a few months to realize a lasting change. Most people see measurable, enduring changes three to six months after they begin working on a skill.

6. **Measure your progress.** Once you've made sufficient progress in the EQ skill you selected for part one of your action plan, go online and take the *Emotional Intelligence Appraisal®* a second time. Complete part two of the action plan.

My EQ Action Plan

Part One – My Journey Begins
Date Completed: _____

List your scores from the Emotional Intelligence Appraisal® test below.

	Score
Overall EQ:	_____
Self-awareness:	_____
Self-management:	_____
Social Awareness:	_____
Relationship Management:	_____

Pick One EQ Skill and Three Strategies

Which of the four core emotional intelligence skills will you work on first? Circle your chosen skill in the image below.

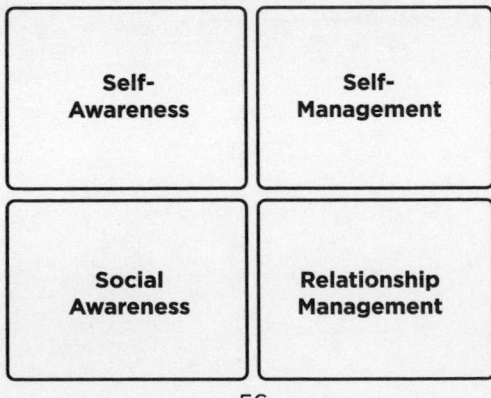

Review the strategies for the EQ skill you selected, and list up to three below that you will practice.

1. _____

_____

2. _____

_____

3. _____

_____

| My EQ Mentor

Who do you know who is gifted in your chosen EQ skill and willing to provide feedback and advice throughout your journey?

My EQ mentor is: _____

Part Two – How Far My Journey Has Come
Date Completed: _____

After you take the Emotional Intelligence Appraisal ® test a second time, list your new and old scores below.

	Old Score	New Score	Change
Overall EQ:	_____	_____	_____
Self-awareness:	_____	_____	_____
Self-management:	_____	_____	_____
Social Awareness:	_____	_____	_____
Relationship Management:	_____	_____	_____

Pick a New EQ Skill and Three Strategies

Based on the results explained in your Emotional Intelligence Appraisal® feedback report, where will you focus your skill development efforts going forward? Pick a new EQ skill and circle it in the image below.

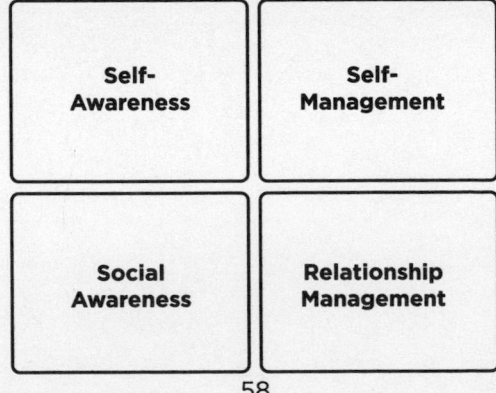

Review the strategies for the EQ skill you selected, and list up to three below that you will practice.

1. _____

_____

2. _____

_____

3. _____

_____

| My New EQ Mentor

Who do you know who is gifted in your new chosen EQ skill and willing to provide feedback and advice throughout your journey?

My new EQ mentor is: _____

5

SELF-AWARENESS STRATEGIES

Simply put, to be self-aware is to know yourself as you really are. Initially, self-awareness can come across as a somewhat ambiguous concept. There is no finish line where someone is going to slap a medal on you and deem you "self-aware." Awareness of yourself is not just knowing that you are a morning person instead of a night owl. It's deeper than that. Getting to know yourself inside and out is a continuous journey of peeling back the layers of the onion and becoming more and more comfortable with what is in the middle—the true essence of you.

Your hard-wired emotional reactions to anything come before you even have a chance to respond. Since it isn't possible to leave your emotions out of the equation, managing yourself and your relationships means you first need to be aware of the full range of your feelings, both positive and negative.

When you don't take time out to notice and understand your emotions, they have a strange way of resurfacing when you least expect or want them to. It's their way of trying to bring something important to your attention. They will persist, and the damage will mount, until you take notice. Facing the truth about who you are can at times be unsettling. Getting in touch with your emotions and tendencies takes honesty and courage. Be patient and give yourself credit for even the smallest bits of forward momentum. As you start noticing things about yourself that you weren't previously aware of (things you aren't always going to like), you are progressing.

The remainder of this chapter introduces you to 15 original strategies, which were designed to help you maximize your self-awareness to create positive changes in your life. The strategies are straightforward and packed full of insights and examples that will help your self-awareness grow.

SELF-AWARENESS STRATEGIES

1. Quit Treating Your Feelings as Good or Bad
2. Observe the Ripple Effect from Your Emotions
3. Lean into Your Discomfort
4. Feel Your Emotions Physically
5. Know Who and What Pushes Your Buttons
6. Watch Yourself Like a Hawk
7. Keep a Journal about Your Emotions
8. Don't Be Fooled by a Bad Mood
9. Don't Be Fooled by a Good Mood, Either
10. Stop and Ask Yourself *Why* You Do the Things You Do
11. Visit Your Values
12. Check Yourself
13. Spot Your Emotions in Books, Movies, and Music
14. Seek Feedback
15. Get to Know Yourself Under Stress

1 Quit Treating Your Feelings as Good or Bad

It's human nature to want to create two simple and easy piles of emotions: the good ones and the bad ones. For instance, most people would automatically classify guilt as *bad*. You don't want to feel it—you might even beat yourself up about it—and you do whatever you can to get rid of it. Likewise, we tend to let good emotions like excitement run wild. We pump ourselves up and feed off the energy.

The downfall of attaching such labels to your emotions is that judging your emotions keeps you from really understanding what it is that you are feeling. When you allow yourself to sit with an emotion and become fully aware of it, you can understand what is causing it. Suspending judgment of emotions allows them to run their course and vanish. Passing judgment on whether you should or shouldn't be feeling what you are feeling just heaps more emotions on top of the pile and prevents the original feeling from running its course.

> **Suspending judgment of emotions allows them to run their course and vanish.**

So, the next time you feel an emotion begin to build, take notice of it immediately. Refrain from putting it into the good or bad pile and remind yourself that the feeling is there to help you understand something important.

2 Observe the Ripple Effect from Your Emotions

Consider for a moment what happens when you drop a stone into water. The stone's swift plummet pierces the water's surface, sending ripples in all directions. Your outpourings of emotion are like stones that send ripples through the people in your life. Since emotions are the primary drivers of your behavior, it's important you understand the effect they have on other people.

Let's say a manager loses his cool and berates an employee in front of the rest of the team. When the lashing happens, it may seem that the manager's target is the only one whose feelings get bruised, but the ripple effect from the manager's explosion affects all who witnessed it. As the rest of the team members wander back to their desks, the others, too, feel the manager's wrath. They go back to work with a pit in their stomachs, each one wondering when his or her turn will come up.

The manager thinks his tirade was good for productivity because the rant "scared people straight," but their fear soon settles into caution. To perform at their best, the team members need to take risks, stretch themselves beyond their comfort zone, and even make some mistakes along the way. No one on the team wants to be the manager's next target, so the team members play it safe and do only as they are told. When the manager gets docked a year later for leading a team that fails to take initiative, he wonders what's wrong with *the team.*

Your emotions are powerful weapons, and continuing to think that their effects are instant and minimal will only do you a disservice. The key to observing the ripple effects of your emotions is to watch closely how they impact other people immediately, and then use that information as a guide for how your emotions are bound to affect a wider circle long after you unleash the emotion. To fully understand the ripple effects of your emotions, you'll need to spend some time reflecting upon your behavior. You'll also need to ask other people how they are affected by your emotions. The more you understand how your emotions ripple outward, the better equipped you'll be to choose the type of ripples that you want to create.

3 Lean into Your Discomfort

The biggest obstacle to increasing your self-awareness is the tendency to avoid the discomfort that comes from seeing yourself as you really are. Things you do not think about are off your radar for a reason: they can sting when they surface. Avoiding this pain creates problems, because it is merely a short-term fix. You'll never be able to manage yourself effectively if you ignore what you need to do to change.

Rather than avoiding a feeling, your goal should be to move toward the emotion, into it, and eventually through it. This can be said for even mild emotional discomfort, such as boredom, confusion, or anticipation. When you ignore or minimize an emotion, no matter how small or insignificant, you miss the opportunity to do something productive with that feeling. Even worse, ignoring your feelings does not make them go away; it just helps them to surface again when you least expect them.

> **Rather than avoiding a feeling, your goal should be to move toward the emotion, into it, and eventually through it.**

To be effective in life, we all need to discover our own

arrogance—those things we don't bother to learn about and dismiss as unimportant. One person thinks apologies are for sissies, so she never learns to recognize when one is needed. Another person hates feeling down, so he constantly distracts himself with meaningless activity and never really feels content. Both people need to take the bold step of leaning into the feelings that will motivate them to change. Otherwise, they will continue down an unproductive, unsatisfying path, repeating the same patterns over and over again.

After the first few times you lean into your discomfort, you will quickly find that the discomfort isn't so bad, it doesn't ruin you, and it reaps rewards. The surprising thing about increasing your self-awareness is that just thinking about it will help you change, even though much of your focus will initially be on the things you do "wrong." Don't be afraid of your emotional "mistakes." They tell you what you should be doing differently and provide the steady stream of information you need to understand yourself as life unfolds.

4 Feel Your Emotions Physically

When you experience an emotion, electric signals course through your brain and trigger physical sensations in your body. The physical sensations can be as varied as your stomach muscles tightening, your heart rate increasing, your breathing quickening, or your mouth going dry. Because your mind and body are so tightly connected, one of the most effective ways to understand your emotions as they are happening is to learn how to spot the physical changes that accompany your emotions.

To better understand the physical effects of your emotions, try closing your eyes the next time you have a few moments alone. Feel how fast or slow your heart is beating. Notice the pace of your breathing. Determine how tense or relaxed the muscles are in your arms, legs, neck, and back. Now, think of a couple of events from your life—one positive and one negative—that generate strong emotions. Think through one of these events in enough detail that you can feel your emotions stir. Take note of the physical changes that accompany the feelings. Do they make your breathing or heart rate change? Do your muscles grow tense? Do you feel hotter or colder? Repeat this process with the other event, and take note of the physical differences in the emotions from the positive and negative experiences.

Closing your eyes and thinking of emotionally arousing events is simply training for the real thing—spotting the physical signs of your emotions on the fly. In the beginning, try not to think too hard—simply open your mind to noticing the sensations. As you improve at this, you'll find that you're often physically aware of an emotion long before you're mentally aware of it.

5 Know Who and What Pushes Your Buttons

We all have buttons—pet peeves, triggers, whatever you want to call them—that, when pushed, just irritate and irk us until we want to scream. Perhaps you have a coworker who lives her life as if she were constantly on stage. Her entrance into meetings is dramatic and flaring, and she feeds off the energy from everyone's attention and uses that energy to take control of the room. Her voice is louder than most, and her contributions to the meetings are always long-winded novels, as if she just loves to hear herself talk.

If your modus operandi is more subtle (or you really would like part of that stage yourself), a person like that may really eat at you. When you go into a meeting with great ideas and a readiness to just sit down and get straight to the point, a drama queen who is creating a stage in the boardroom is bound to flip your switches for frustration and rage. Even if you aren't the type to blurt out impulsive comments or otherwise go on the attack, your body language may give you away, or you may find yourself on the drive home obsessing over your lingering frustration.

Knowing who pushes your buttons and how they do it is critical to developing the ability to take control of these situations, maintain your poise, and calm yourself down. To use this strategy, you can't think about things generally. You need to pinpoint the specific people and situations that trigger your emotions. Your buttons are bound to get pushed by a wide range of people and things. It could be certain people (like drama queens), particular situations (like feeling scared or caught off guard), or conditions in the environment (like noisy offices). Having a clear understanding of who and what pushes your buttons makes these people and situations a bit less difficult because they come as less of a surprise.

You can take your self-awareness a big step further by discovering the source of your buttons. That is, why do these people and situations irk you so much when other, equally annoying people and situations don't bother you at all? Perhaps the stage hog reminds you of your sister who got all the attention when you were younger. You lived many years in her shadow, vowing to never let it happen again. Now you sit beside her clone in every meeting. No wonder she's a trigger for your emotions.

Knowing why your buttons are what they are opens doors to managing your reactions to your triggers. For now, your tasks are simple—find the sources of your buttons and jot down a list. Knowing your buttons is essential to using the self and relationship management strategies that come later in the book.

6 Watch Yourself Like a Hawk

Hawks have the distinct advantage of soaring hundreds of feet above the ground, looking down upon the Earth and seeing all that happens below them. The creatures on the ground go about their lives with narrow tunnel vision, not even realizing that the hawk is soaring above them predicting their every move. Wouldn't it be great to be the hawk, looking down upon yourself in those sticky situations that tend to get the better of you? Think of all the things you would be able to see and understand from above. Your objectivity would allow you to step out from under the control of your emotions and know exactly what needed to be done to create a positive outcome.

Even though you are not a hawk, you can still develop a more objective understanding of your own behavior. You can practice by taking notice of your emotions, thoughts, and behaviors right as the situation unfolds. In essence, the goal is to slow yourself down and take in all that is in front of you, allowing your brain to process all available information before you act.

Consider an example. Let's say you have a teenage son who is more than two hours late for his Friday night curfew. You're sitting in a living room chair in the dark, waiting for him to stroll through the door and offer another creative explanation for why he's late and wasn't answering his phone. The more you sit there thinking about your son's disregard for your authority and the hours of sleep he's just robbed you of, the more your blood boils. Before long, you've forgotten the real reason you're so upset—you're worried about his safety. Sure, you want him to obey the rules, but it's the thought of him out there acting recklessly that's keeping you up.

Watching yourself like a hawk in this situation requires taking advantage of this calm before the storm. You know your anger is going to rumble to the surface the moment his weak excuses tumble from his mouth, and you also know he's more likely to follow your rules if you can get him to see and feel your concern. This is the moment when you need to consider what this situation looks like from above. You realize your brooding is just fanning the flames of your anger. You remember that he's a good kid who's been acting too much like a typical teenager lately. You know your anger isn't going to make him change; it hasn't worked thus far. The bigger picture now in clear view, you decide to explain the rationale for his punishment and why you are so upset, rather than just fly off the handle. When he finally comes slithering into the house, knocking the lamp off the end table in the darkness, you're grateful you can see the whole picture and not just what's in front of you.

7 Keep a Journal about Your Emotions

The biggest challenge to developing self-awareness is objectivity. It's hard to develop perspective on your emotions and tendencies when every day feels like a new mountain to climb.

The biggest challenge to developing self-awareness is objectivity.

With a journal, you can record what events triggered strong emotions in you and how you responded to them.

You should write about time spent at work and home—nothing is off limits. In just a month, you'll begin to see patterns in your emotions, and you'll develop a better understanding of your tendencies. You'll get a better idea of which emotions get you down, which pick you up, and which are the most difficult for you to tolerate. Pay careful attention to the people and situations that push your buttons, triggering strong emotions. Describe the emotions you feel each day, and don't forget to record the physical sensations that accompany the emotions.

In addition to helping you see yourself more clearly, writing down your emotions makes your tendencies much easier to remember, and the journal serves as a great reference as you raise your self-awareness.

8 Don't Be Fooled by a Bad Mood

We all succumb to them every now and then—those down-in-the-dumps moods where nothing seems to be going our way. When you feel this way, your low mood puts a dark cloud over every thought, feeling, and experience you have. The tricky thing about your brain is that, once a negative mood takes over, you lose sight of what's good in your life, and suddenly you hate your job, you're frustrated with family and friends, you're dissatisfied with your accomplishments, and your optimism about the future goes out the window. Deep down, you know that things aren't as bad as they seem, but your brain just won't hear it.

Part of self-awareness is knowing what you're going through even if you can't totally change it. Admit to yourself that your bad mood is hanging a cloud over everything you see, and remind yourself that your moods are not permanent. Your emotions change all the time, and low moods will pass if you allow them to.

When you're stuck in a down mood, it's not a good time to make important decisions. You'll have to remain aware of the mood and understand it if you hope to keep it from leading you to make mistakes that will only pull you down further. Not only is it OK to reflect upon recent events that may have brought on the mood, but this is also a good idea—as long as you don't dwell on them for too long—because often that's all it takes to get the mood to pass.

9 Don't Be Fooled by a Good Mood, Either

Bad moods and negative emotions are not the only ones that cause trouble. A good mood can deceive your thinking just as much as a bad one. When you are feeling excited and really happy, it's easy to do something that you'll regret.

Consider this familiar scenario: your favorite store is having a once-a-year sale with markdowns of up to 75%. You rush into the store on the day of the sale and end up buying all sorts of things that you've always wanted but can't really afford (at least not all at once). The rush and exhilaration of your purchases carry you through the week as you show off the goods to your friends and family and let them in on the fabulous deals you got. When your credit card bill arrives at the end of the month, it's another story.

Foolish spending is not the only mistake you can make while riding the high of a great mood. The excitement and energy you enjoy during a good mood paint a rosy picture of all you encounter. This leaves you far more likely to make impulsive decisions that ignore the potential consequences of your actions. Stay aware of your good moods and the foolish decisions these moods can lead to, and you'll be able to enjoy feeling good without any regrets.

10 Stop and Ask Yourself *Why* You Do the Things You Do

Emotions come when they will, not when you will them to. Your self-awareness will grow abundantly when you begin seeking out the source of your feelings. Get in the habit of stopping to ask yourself why surprising emotions rumbled to the surface and what motivated you to do something out of character. Emotions serve an important purpose—they clue you into things that you'll never understand if you don't take the time to ask yourself why.

Most of the time, it really is that easy, but when you are left to your own devices, the days can just whiz by with little time to contemplate why you do what you do. With a little practice, you can trace your emotional reactions back to their origins and understand the purpose of your emotions. The surprising thing about this strategy is that just paying attention to your emotions and asking yourself good questions like these are enough to help you improve. Can you remember the first time you reacted like this and with whom? Are there similarities between then and now? Can anyone evoke this reaction in you or only specific people? The better you understand why you do the things you do, the better equipped you'll be to keep your emotions from running the show.

11 Visit Your Values

The plates of life are constantly spinning above you. You juggle projects at work, never-ending meetings, bills, errands, emails, phone calls, text messages, chores, meals, time with friends and family—the list goes on. It takes great amounts of attention and focus to keep the plates from crashing to the ground.

Maintaining this balancing act keeps your attention focused outward, rather than inward and on yourself. As you run around struggling to check your daily "to dos" off your list, it's easy to lose sight of what's really important to you—your core values and beliefs. Before you know it, you find yourself doing and saying things that deep down you don't feel good about or believe in. This could mean you find yourself yelling at a coworker who made a mistake, when you normally find such hostility unacceptable. If yelling at your colleagues runs contrary to the beliefs you wish to live your life by, catching yourself (or being caught) doing it is bound to make you uncomfortable and even unfulfilled.

The trick here is to take the time to check in with yourself and jot down your core beliefs and values. Ask yourself, *what are the values that I wish to live my life by?* Take a sheet of paper and separate it into two columns. List your core values and beliefs in the left column and anything that you've done or said recently that you aren't proud of in the right column. Is what you value in alignment with the manner in which you conduct yourself? If not, consider alternatives to what you said and did that would have made you proud of yourself, or at least more comfortable.

Repeating this exercise somewhere between daily and monthly will be a huge boost to your self-awareness. Before long, you'll find yourself thinking of the list *before* you act, which will set the stage for making choices you can live with.

12 Check Yourself

Self-awareness is generally an internal process, but there are a few instances in which the outside holds the clues you need to understand what's going on inside. Without question, how you feel is reflected in how you look. Your facial expressions, posture, demeanor, clothes, and even your hair all say important things about your mood.

Physical appearance is more straightforward—what you wear sends a pretty clear, established message about how you feel. For example, wearing old sweatpants and ratty T-shirts and having disheveled hair every day tells the world you've given up, while overdressing for every occasion and never missing your weekly haircut lets people know you are trying too hard. Your demeanor also says a lot about your mood, but the message often gets twisted. If you're meeting someone for the first time and you're feeling insecure about how you'll be received, like many people, you may tend to be aloof and a bit standoffish or get overzealous.

When you find yourself in similar situations, it's important to notice your mood and consider its influence upon your demeanor. Is the look that you are projecting to the world one that you have chosen, one that your mood created, or one that you tend to lean on by default? Certainly, what you project reflects how you feel, and it's up to you to understand it. Taking a moment here and there to check yourself will allow you to understand your mood *before* it sets the tone for the rest of your day.

13 Spot Your Emotions in Books, Movies, and Music

If you're having trouble looking within to spot your emotional patterns and tendencies, you can discover the same information by looking outside yourself at the movies, music, and books that you identify with. When the lyrics or mood of a song resonate with you, they say a lot about how you feel, and when a character from a movie or book sticks in your head, it's probably because important aspects of his or her thoughts and feelings parallel your own. Taking a closer look in these moments can teach you a lot about yourself. It can also provide a great tool for explaining your feelings to other people.

Finding your emotions in the expressions of artists allows you to learn about yourself and discover feelings that are often hard to communicate. Sometimes you just can't find the words to say what you are feeling until you see it in front of you. Listening to music, reading novels, watching films, and even looking at art can act as a gateway into your deepest emotions. Take a closer look the next time one of these mediums grabs your attention—you never know what you'll find.

14 Seek Feedback

Everything you see—including yourself—must travel through your own lens. The problem is, your lens is tainted by your experiences, your beliefs, and, without question, your moods. Your lens prevents you from ever obtaining a truly objective look at yourself, on your own. Often, there is a big difference between how you see yourself and how others see you. This chasm between the way you view yourself and the way others view you is a rich source of lessons that will build your self-awareness.

> **Self-awareness is the process of getting to know yourself from the inside out and the outside in.**

Self-awareness is the process of getting to know yourself from the inside out and the outside in. The only way to get the second, more elusive perspective is to open yourself up to feedback from others, which can include friends, coworkers, mentors, supervisors, and family. When you ask for their feedback, be sure to get specific examples and situations, and as you gather the answers, look for similarities in the information. Others' views can be a real eye-opener by showing you how other people experience *you*. Putting the perspectives together helps you see the entire picture, including how your emotions and reactions affect other people. By mustering the courage to peer at what others see, you can reach a level of self-awareness that few people attain.

15 Get to Know Yourself Under Stress

The mountain of stressors in your life is constantly growing. Every time your stress tolerance rises to new heights, you—or those around you—push and push until you take on more. All of the high-tech gadgets at your disposal aren't helping, either. If anything, they just seem to speed up your life. If you are like most people, you already recognize some of the warning signs that pop up when stress is looming. The question is: do you heed their warning?

You will benefit tremendously from learning to recognize your first signs of stress. The human mind and body— at least when it comes to stress—have voices of their own. They tell you through emotional and physiological reactions when it's time to slow down and take a break. For example, an upset stomach can be a sign that nervousness and anxiety are overwhelming your body. The indigestion and fatigue that follow are your body's way of taking some time off to rest. For you, intense stress and anxiety may create an upset stomach, while for others the physical signs can be a pounding headache, canker sores, or their backs going out. Your self-awareness in times of stress should serve as your third ear to listen to your body's cries for help. Your body speaks volumes when you push it too hard.

Take the time to recognize these signals and recharge your emotional battery before your stress causes permanent damage to your system.

6

—

SELF-MANAGEMENT STRATEGIES

Self-management is your ability to use awareness of your emotions to actively choose what you say and do. On the surface, it may seem that self-management is simply a matter of taking a deep breath and keeping yourself in check when emotions come on strong, and while it's true that self-control in these situations is a sizeable piece of the pie, there's far more to self-management than putting a cork in it when you're about to blow up. Your eruptions are no different from a volcano—there is all sorts of rumbling happening beneath the surface before the lava starts flowing.

Unlike a volcano, there are subtle things you can do each and every day to influence what is happening beneath the surface. You just need to learn how to pick up on the rumbling and respond to it. Self-management builds upon a foundational skill—self-awareness. Ample self-awareness is necessary for effective self-management because you can only choose how to respond to an emotion actively when you're aware of it. Since we're hard-wired to experience emotions before we can respond to them, it's the one-two punch of reading emotions effectively and then reacting to them that sets the best self-managers apart. A high level of self-management ensures you aren't getting in your own way and doing things that limit your success. It also ensures you aren't frustrating other people to the point that they resent or dislike you. When you understand your own emotions and can respond to them the way you choose to, you have the power to take control of difficult situations, react nimbly to change, and take the initiative needed to achieve your goals.

When you develop the ability to size yourself up quickly and grab the reins before you head in the wrong direction, it keeps you flexible and allows you to choose positively and productively how to react to different situations. When you don't stop to think about your feelings—including how they are influencing your behavior now, and will continue to do so in the future—you set yourself up to be a frequent victim of emotional hijackings. Whether you're aware of it or not, your emotions will control you, and you'll move through your day reacting to your feelings with little choice in what you say and do.

The remainder of this chapter presents 17 specific strategies—things you can start doing today—that will help you manage your emotions to your benefit. Each simple strategy is targeted to an important element of the self-management skill. This carefully crafted set has been honed through many years of testing with people just like you, and are proven methods for increasing your self-management skill.

As you master each of the strategies and incorporate them into your daily routine, you will develop an increased capacity to respond effectively to your emotions. Of course no matter how skilled you become in managing your emotions there are always going to be situations that push your buttons. Your life won't morph into a fairy tale devoid of obstacles, but you *will* equip yourself with everything you need to take the wheel and drive.

SELF-MANAGEMENT STRATEGIES

1. Breathe Right
2. Create an Emotion vs. Reason List
3. Make Your Goals Public
4. Count to Ten
5. Sleep on It
6. Talk to a Skilled Self-Manager
7. Smile and Laugh More
8. Set Aside Some Time in Your Day for Problem Solving
9. Take Control of Your Self-Talk
10. Visualize Yourself Succeeding
11. Clean Up Your Sleep Hygiene
12. Focus Your Attention on Your Freedoms, Rather than Your Limitations
13. Stay Synchronized
14. Speak to Someone Who Is *Not* Emotionally Invested in Your Problem
15. Learn a Valuable Lesson from Everyone You Encounter
16. Put a Mental Recharge into Your Schedule
17. Accept That Change Is Just around the Corner

1 Breathe Right

If you're like most people, you breathe in short, shallow breaths throughout the day that don't fully contract your diaphragm to fill your lungs—and you don't even know it. What's to stop you? It's not like you are suffering from the lack of oxygen . . . or so you think. Your lungs are built to provide *precisely* the amount of air your body needs for *all* of your organs to function effectively. When you take a shallow breath—which is any breath that fails to make your stomach protrude outward from the influx of air—you aren't giving your body the full amount of oxygen it needs.

Your brain demands a full 20 percent of your body's oxygen supply, which it needs to control basic functions like breathing and sight and complex functions like thinking and managing your mood. Your brain dedicates oxygen first to the basic functions, because they keep you alive. Whatever oxygen remains is used for the complex functions, which keep you alert, focused, and calm. Shallow breaths deprive your brain of oxygen, which can lead to poor concentration, forgetfulness, mood swings, restlessness, depressed and anxious thoughts, and a lack of energy. Shallow breathing handicaps your ability to self-manage.

The next time you are in a stressful or emotional situation, focus on taking slow deep breaths, inhaling through your nose until you can feel your stomach swell outward and grow tight, and then exhaling gently and completely through your mouth. As you exhale, go ahead and push that breath out until you have completely emptied your lungs. If you want to make sure that you are breathing correctly, place one hand upon your sternum (the long, flat bone located in the center of your chest) and the other hand upon your stomach as you take in breaths. If the hand on your stomach is moving more than the hand on your sternum as you exhale, then you know that you're getting enough oxygen and fully inflating your lungs. If you practice this proper breathing technique, it will grow comfortable enough that you can do it in the presence of other people without them noticing, which is handy for when you find yourself in the middle of a difficult conversation.

Anytime you choose to breathe right and flood your brain with oxygen, you'll notice the effects immediately. Many people describe the sensation as one of entering a calmer, more relaxed state where they have a clear head. This makes breathing right one of the simplest yet most powerful techniques that you have at your disposal to manage your emotions. In addition to engaging your rational brain on the spot, breathing right is a great tool for shifting your focus away from intruding, uncomfortable thoughts that are hard to shake. Whether you are overcome by anxiety and stress because of a looming deadline, or fixated on negative thoughts and feelings about something that happened in the past, making yourself breathe right calms you down and makes you feel better by powering up your rational brain.

2 Create an Emotion vs. Reason List

You may not always realize it, but there are many times when you allow your emotions to sway you in one direction while your rational mind is tugging at your shirt to go another way. Whenever you find your mind having a battle of the brains (emotional vs. rational), it's time to make a list that distinguishes the emotional side of the argument from the rational one. The list will allow you to clear your mind, use your knowledge and take into account the importance of your emotions without letting them take control.

Creating an Emotion vs. Reason list is simple. Draw a straight line down the middle of a page to make two columns. In the left column write what your emotions are telling you to do, and in the right column what your reason is telling you to do. Now, ask yourself two important questions: Where are your emotions clouding your judgment, and where is your reason ignoring important cues from your emotions? Your emotions will create trouble if you let them lead you around without any reason, but your rational thoughts can be just as problematic if you try to operate like a robot that is without feeling. Your feelings are there whether you acknowledge them or not, and the Emotion vs. Reason list forces you to get in touch with them by putting them down on paper.

So, the next time a sticky or stressful situation gives you grief, grab a sheet of paper and give yourself a few quiet moments to organize your thoughts and make your list. With the list in front of you, it will be much easier to see whether you should allow the emotional or rational sides of your thinking to have more say in your decision.

3 Make Your Goals Public

Walking your talk is hard, especially when life is always throwing you curveballs. Sometimes, the biggest letdowns are private ones—when we fail to reach a goal or do what we set out to do. There is no more powerful motivator to reach your goals than making them public. If you clearly tell other people what you are setting out to accomplish—be it friends, family or a spouse—their awareness of your progress creates an incredible sense of accountability.

Much of self-management comes down to motivation, and you can use the expectations that other people have of you as a powerful force to get you up off the proverbial couch. If your boss assigns a project or your running partner meets you every morning at 5 a.m. sharp, you're simply more likely to do something when other people are involved. Select those people whom you know will actually pay attention to your

> **Much of self-management comes down to motivation, and you can use the expectations that other people have of you as a powerful force to get you up off the proverbial couch.**

progress. When you share your goals with others, ask them to monitor your progress and hold you accountable. You may even give them the power to dole out reward or punishment, such as the university professor we know who pays his colleagues $100 anytime he misses a deadline on a research article. As you can imagine, he is the rare individual who hardly ever misses a deadline!

4 Count to Ten

You can thank your kindergarten teacher for this one! It was way back then sitting on the classroom rug with your legs crossed that you learned one of the most effective strategies for turning the temperature down when your emotions are running hot. Adulthood has a funny way of making us lose sight of some simple, yet profound, strategies for self-control.

All you have to do is this: When you feel yourself getting frustrated or angry, stop yourself by taking in a deep breath and saying the number one to yourself as you exhale. Keep breathing and counting until you reach the number ten. The counting and breathing will relax you and stop you from taking rash action long enough to regain your composure and develop a more clear, rational perspective of the situation.

Sometimes, you might not even reach ten. For example, if you are in a meeting and someone abruptly interrupts you to blurt out something ridiculous that rubs you raw, you are unlikely to sit there silently while you breathe your way to ten. Even if you don't make it to double digits, you'll stop the flow of frustration and anger long enough to cool down your overheated limbic system and give your rational brain some valuable time to catch up.

When your counting needs to be more subtle, there are lots of great ways to hide it from others. Some people will actually bring a beverage with them to every meeting they attend. This way, whenever they feel as though they may blurt out some emotionally charged statement, they take a drink. No one expects them to talk when they are drinking. So they have the time they need to calm down (and count if necessary), organize their thoughts, and plan something to say that's more constructive.

> **Even if you don't make it to double digits, you'll stop the flow of frustration and anger long enough to cool down your overheated limbic system and give your rational brain some valuable time to catch up.**

Reacting quickly and without much thought fans the flames burning in the emotional brain. Since a snappy comeback usually leads to a heated exchange where barbs are thrown back and forth, it's easy to find yourself in the midst of a full-blown emotional hijacking. When you slow things down and focus on counting, it engages your rational brain. You can then regain control of yourself and keep your emotions from running the show.

5 Sleep on It

In the timeless classic, *War and Peace*, Leo Tolstoy wrote that the two strongest warriors are time and patience. The power of these warriors comes from their ability to transform situations, ease pain, and provide clarity. Sometimes situations that require our patience can feel so uncomfortable, dissatisfying, and rife with anxiety that we jump to action just to alleviate the internal turmoil. But more often than not, giving yourself that extra day, week, or month to digest the situation before moving forward is all you need to stay in control. And sometimes, while you're waiting, things may surface that make your decision that much easier to make.

Time helps you to self-manage because it brings clarity and perspective to the thousands of thoughts that go swimming through your head when something is important. Time also helps you to gain control of emotions that you know would lead you in the wrong direction if you were to let them drive. It's that simple. All you need to do is force yourself to wait for the dust to settle before you make a move.

6 Talk to a Skilled Self-Manager

Role models come in all shapes and sizes, and they influence our lives in ways that are hard to predict. One of the most powerful ways to learn self-management is to seek out skilled self-managers to learn their tricks.

Most people's weaknesses in emotional intelligence are simply the product of skills that don't come naturally to them. In the case of people who are gifted in an emotional intelligence skill, they are usually very aware of what it is they do well, which makes it easy for you to learn from them.

First, find a person whom you consider to be a master self-manager. If you don't feel that you can spot a skilled self-manager on your own, you can always have someone take the test that comes with this book. Offer to take your self-management whiz out for lunch or coffee, explain that you are seeking improvement in this skill, and ask him or her to review the self-management section of this book before the meeting. During the meeting share your specific goals for improved self-management, and ask what tactics he or she relies on to self-manage so well. Be sure to share the emotions and situations that give you the most trouble. You're bound to learn some unique and effective ways to manage yourself that you would have otherwise never been exposed to. Before you leave the meeting, write down the best tips and choose a couple that you can begin trying immediately. Ask your self-management whiz if the two of you can meet again after you've had a chance to try the suggestions out.

7 Smile and Laugh More

Did you know that when you laugh and smile, your face sends signals to your brain that you are happy? Your brain literally responds to the nerves and muscles in your face to determine your emotional state. So what does this mean for self-management? When you're stuck on a frustrating or distressing thought, forcing yourself to smile counteracts the negative emotional state. If you work in customer service, or any time you need to look upbeat when you're really not up for it, making yourself throw on a large, legitimate smile (where your cheeks push upwards) will trick your mind into feeling the mood you need for the moment.

French university researchers measured the power of a smile by having two groups of subjects read the same comics page from the newspaper. One group of subjects was instructed to hold a pencil in their teeth while reading (which activates the muscles used in smiling), while the other group held the pencil with their lips (which does not activate the muscles used in smiling). Those who were unknowingly "smiling" found the cartoons far more humorous and had a better time while reading them than people in the group that weren't smiling.

You can also use smiling and laughter to lift your mood by

watching a show or reading a book that you know you find funny. This can feel like an odd choice when you're feeling down, but it's a great way to override the negative emotions and clear your head, especially if your down mood is paralyzing your judgment. Smiling and laughter won't eliminate feeling down, and they shouldn't—every mood has

> **It's nice to know you have an out when you need to put on a happy face.**

its purpose—but it's nice to know you have an out when you need to put on a happy face.

8 Set Aside Some Time in Your Day for Problem Solving

You experience hundreds of emotions every day, some of which you are not even aware. You spend your day bouncing around from feeling to feeling, which can lead to making some decisions at inopportune times.

Think back through some of your recent decisions, and you'll likely find that the decisions you made while hurrying through your day were seldom as effective as those made with some planning and clear thinking. The only way to ensure that you have the right space to make good decisions is to set aside some time in your schedule for problem solving. Just keep it simple. A 15-minute period each day where you turn off your phone, walk away from your computer, and take time to just think, is a great way to ensure your decisions aren't muddled by your emotions.

9 Take Control of Your Self-Talk

Research suggests the average person has about 50,000 thoughts every day. Sound like a lot? It doesn't stop there. Every time one of those 50,000 thoughts takes place, chemicals are produced in your brain that can trigger reactions felt throughout your body. There is a strong relationship between what you think and how you feel, both physically and emotionally. Because you are always thinking (much like breathing), you tend to forget that you are doing it. You likely don't even realize how much your thoughts dictate how you feel every hour of every single day.

It's impossible to try and track every single thought you have to see if it's having a positive or negative influence on your emotional state. The thoughts that are most influential are those where you literally talk to yourself. Though you might not realize you have these thoughts, we all have an internal voice inside our head that affects our perception of things. We tell ourselves to keep quiet, we congratulate ourselves on a job well done and we reprimand ourselves for making poor decisions. Our thoughts are "talking" to us every day, and this inner voice is called "self-talk."

With thoughts—your primary vehicles for regulating your

emotional flow—what you allow yourself to think can rumble emotions to the surface, stuff them down underground, and intensify and prolong any emotional experience. When a rush of emotion comes over you, your thoughts turn the heat up or down. By learning to control your self-talk, you can keep yourself focused on the right things and manage your emotions more effectively.

Much of the time, your self-talk is positive and it helps you through your day ("I'd better get ready for the meeting" or "I'm really looking forward to going out to dinner tonight"). Your self-talk damages your ability to self-manage anytime it becomes negative. Negative self-talk is unrealistic and self-defeating. It can send you into a downward emotional spiral that makes it difficult to get what you want from life.

What follow are the most common types of negative self-talk with the keys to taking control of them and turning them around:

1. **Turn *I always* or *I never* into just *this time* or *sometimes*.** Your actions are unique to the situation in front of you, no matter how often you think you mess up. Make certain your thoughts follow suit. When you start treating each situation as its own animal and stop beating yourself up over every mistake, you'll stop making your problems bigger than they really are.

2. **Replace judgmental statements like *I'm an idiot* with factual ones like *I made a mistake*.** Thoughts that attach a permanent label to you leave no room for improvement. Factual statements are objective, situational, and help you to focus on what you can change.

3. **Accept responsibility for your actions and no one else's.** The blame game and negative self-talk go hand in hand. If you are someone who often thinks either *it's all my fault* or *it's all their fault* you are wrong most the time. It is commendable to accept responsibility for your actions, but not when you carry someone else's burden. Likewise, if you're always blaming others, it's time to take responsibility for your part.

10 Visualize Yourself Succeeding

This is another strategy that at first glance may appear too simple to be effective, but it packs a powerful punch. Learning to self-manage well requires a lot of practice. Yet, many of the situations that pose the greatest difficulty for you don't come up all that often. So, you'll have a hard time forming the neural pathways needed to make your new skills habitual . . . unless you learn to visualize.

Your brain has a difficult time distinguishing between what you see with your eyes and what you visualize in your mind. In fact, MRI scans of people's brains taken while they are watching the sun set are virtually indistinguishable from scans taken when the same people visualize a sunset in their mind. The same brain regions are active in both scenarios.

Visualizing yourself managing your emotions and behavior effectively is a great way to practice your new skills and make them into habits. For this to work, you might want to do your visualization in a room that's free from distractions, as you'll need to immerse yourself fully in the scenes playing out in your head. A great time to visualize is before you go to bed at night. Just close your eyes and visualize yourself in situations where you have the most difficulty managing yourself. Focus on the details of each situation that make it so hard for you to remain in control; concentrate on the sights and sounds you would experience if you were actually there until you literally feel the same emotions. Next, picture yourself acting the way you'd like to (e.g., calming your nerves and proceeding confidently during a big presentation, dealing with someone who pushes your buttons without losing your cool, etc.). Imagine yourself doing and saying the right things and allow yourself to feel the satisfaction and positive emotions that come from this. Not a bad way to end the day, don't you think? Use this strategy nightly and incorporate new, challenging situations as they surface.

11 Clean Up Your Sleep Hygiene

Self-management requires patience, flexibility, and alertness, which are the first things to go when you don't get a good night's sleep. Getting more sleep at night will probably help you manage yourself better, but not necessarily. The critical factor for an alert, focused, and balanced mind is the quality of your sleep, and for quality sleep you need good sleep hygiene.

While you sleep, your brain literally recharges, shuffling through the day's memories and storing or discarding them (which causes dreams), so that you wake up alert and clearheaded. Your brain is very fickle when it comes to sleep. It needs to move through an elaborate series of cycles for you to wake feeling rested. You can help this along and improve the quality of your sleep by following these steps for good sleep hygiene:

1. **Get twenty minutes of morning sunlight.** Your eyes need at least twenty minutes of pre-noon sunlight (cloudy days are fine) to reset your inner clock, which makes it easier to fall asleep in the evening. The light can't be filtered by windows or sunglasses. So, take the glasses off and crack your car windows on the way to work, or find some time to get outdoors before lunchtime.

2. **Turn off the computer at least two hours before bedtime.** The light of a computer screen right in front of your face late at night is similar enough to sunlight that it tricks your brain, making it difficult to fall asleep and disruptive to the quality of your sleep.

3. **Keep your bed for sleeping.** The best way to check out the moment you hit the mattress is to avoid working or watching television in bed. Save your bed for sleep and your body will respond.

4. **Avoid caffeine, especially in the p.m.** Caffeine has a six-hour half-life. Have a cup of joe at eight a.m., and you'll still have 25 percent of the caffeine in your body at eight p.m. Caffeine keeps you from falling asleep and is extremely disruptive to the quality of your sleep. It's best avoided all together, or at least taken in small amounts and only before noon.

12 Focus Your Attention on Your Freedoms, Rather than Your Limitations

Life isn't fair . . . there's nothing you can do about it . . . it isn't up to you. Moms and dads tend to beat these mantras into their children's heads as if there were some secret Mommy and Daddy Handbook that instructed them to do so. What your folks forgot to explain is that you always have a choice—a choice in how you respond to what's before you. Even when you can't do or say anything to change a difficult situation, you always have a say in your perspective of what's happening, which ultimately influences your feelings about it.

Many times you can't change a situation or even the parties involved, but that doesn't mean it's time for you to give up. When you find yourself thinking that you have no control, take a closer look at how you are reacting to the situation itself. Focusing on restrictions is not only demoralizing—it helps negative feelings surface that confirm your sense of helplessness. You must take accountability for what you have control over, and focus your energy on remaining flexible and open-minded in spite of the situation.

117

13 Stay Synchronized

FBI agents spend much of their time trying to figure out whether suspects are lying. They study body language, voice inflections, and eye contact. The biggest clue that someone is lying occurs when synchrony—body language that matches the emotions being expressed—is absent.

Synchrony is also an important tool for effective self-managers. When you are doing a good job of managing your emotions, your body language will fit the emotional tone of the situation. When you can't keep your body language in check, it is a clear sign that your emotions are getting the best of you.

When a commercial airliner crash-landed safely in New York's Hudson River in 2009, the pilot, Chesley "Sully" Sullenberger, saved every soul onboard by making sure the plane hit the water at the exact angle and speed needed to avoid breaking up upon impact. To accomplish this, he silenced the alarm bells going off in his head and the fear he was feeling. He kept his composure by directing his attention away from fear and onto landing the plane. He kept his emotions from taking the controls, even though he knew the chances for survival were slim.

On most days, you won't be crash-landing airplanes, but, if you're like most people, you'll have moments where your emotions are getting the better of you. To keep yourself synchronized, direct your attention away from your emotions and on to the task at hand.

14 Speak to Someone Who Is *Not* Emotionally Invested in Your Problem

When problems arise, your brain is constantly thinking, constantly sorting and analyzing information to decide the best course of action. The problem is, the only information your brain has to go on is what you've given it—what you've seen before and what's happening now. The way our minds are structured, it's far too easy to get stuck in a single train of thought. Allow this to happen and you're severely limiting your options.

It's no wonder that it can be such a relief to talk to someone when you are feeling confused or emotional about a situation. Not only is it helpful to talk to someone who cares about how you are feeling, but new perspectives open up additional avenues for you to explore.

When a difficult situation surfaces, seek out someone whom you trust and feel comfortable with who is not personally affected by your situation. Use this person as a sounding board for what you've experienced and what you are thinking and feeling about the troubling situation. Their unique perspective will help you to see things differently, and expand your options.

Choose your third party wisely. The people you invite to help you shouldn't have a vested interest in the situation. The more your "counselors" are personally affected by the situation, the more their perspectives are going to be tainted by their own needs and feelings. The opinions of people directly affected by your situation will only muddy the waters for you and should be avoided at all costs. You should also avoid someone you know will simply agree with you. While their support feels good, it keeps you from seeing the entire picture. Sitting down with a potential devil's advocate may irk you in the moment, but you'll fare far better having seen things from a unique perspective.

Self-Management Strategies

15 Learn a Valuable Lesson from Everyone You Encounter

Think back to a time when a conversation immediately put you on the defensive. There you were, forcefully gripping your sword and shield, ready to do battle. Maybe someone criticized you, or a colleague disagreed with you strongly, or perhaps someone questioned your motives. As odd as it may sound, in moments like these you are missing out on a valuable opportunity to learn from other people. Approaching everyone you encounter as though they have something valuable to teach you—something that you will benefit from—is the best way to remain flexible, open-minded, and *much* less stressed.

You can do this with pretty much any situation that happens in your life. Let's say you are driving to work and someone cuts you off and then swerves around a corner and motors off in another direction. Even this inconsiderate jerk has something to teach you. Perhaps you need to learn to have more patience with irritating people. Or it may make you grateful that you are not in such a hurry. It is much more difficult to get angry, defensive, and stressed when you are trying to learn something from the other party.

The next time you find yourself caught off-guard and on the defensive, embrace this opportunity to learn something.

Whether you learn from the other person's feedback, or just from how they are behaving, keeping this perspective is the key to keeping yourself in control.

16 Put a Mental Recharge into Your Schedule

The physical benefits of exercise are obvious, and there always seems to be someone—a doctor, a friend, an article—reminding us that we need to do it more. What most people don't realize is how critical exercise and other relaxing and recharging activities are to the mind. If you want to become an adept self-manager, you need to give your mind a fighting chance, and a lot of this, surprisingly, comes down to how you treat your body.

When you take time out of your day to get your blood flowing and keep your body healthy, it gives your mind an important break—the most significant rest and recharge you can give your brain beyond sleep. While intense physical activity is ideal, other more relaxing and equally invigorating diversions can also have a great effect on your mind. Yoga, massage, gardening or a stroll through the park are all relaxing ways to give your mind a breather. These activities—though none more so than vigorous exercise—release chemicals in your brain like serotonin and endorphins that recharge it and help to keep you happy and alert. They also engage and strengthen areas in your brain that are responsible for good decision-making, planning, organization, and rational thinking.

For most of us the biggest challenge in implementing this strategy is finding the time to squeeze these things into our day. They tend to tumble down our priority list as work, family, and friends monopolize our days. If you recognize recharging your mind for what it is—a maintenance activity that's as important to your brain as brushing your teeth is for your mouth—it's easier to schedule it into your calendar at the start of the week, rather than waiting to see if you find the time. If you want to improve your self-management skills, implementing this strategy will be well worth the effort.

17 Accept That Change Is Just around the Corner

None of us are born with a crystal ball that predicts the future. Since you can't foresee every change and every obstacle that life throws in your path, the key to navigating change successfully is your perspective *before* changes even surface.

The idea here is to prepare for change. This is not so much a guessing game where you test your accuracy in anticipating what's next, but rather thinking through the consequences of potential changes so that you aren't caught off guard if they surface. The first step is to admit to yourself that even the most stable, trusted facets of your life are not completely under your control. People change, businesses go through ebbs and flows, and things just don't stay the same for long. When you allow yourself to anticipate change—and understand your options if changes occur—you prevent yourself from getting bogged down by strong emotions like shock, surprise, fear and disappointment when changes actually happen. While you're still likely to experience these negative emotions, your

> **Admit to yourself that even the most stable, trusted facets of your life are not completely under your control.**

acceptance that change is an inevitable part of life enables you to focus and think rationally, which is critical to making the most out of an unlikely, unwanted or otherwise unforeseen situation.

The best way to implement this strategy fully is to set aside a small amount of time either every week or every other week to create a list of important changes that you think could *possibly* happen. These are the changes you'll want to be prepared for. Leave enough room below each change on your list to write out all the possible actions you will take should the change occur. And below that, jot down ideas for things that you can do now to prepare for that change. What are the signs that you can keep an eye out for that would suggest the change is imminent? Should you see these signs, is there anything you can do to prepare and soften the blow? Even if the changes on your list never come to fruition, just anticipating change and knowing what you'd do in response to it makes you a more flexible and adaptive person overall.

7

SOCIAL AWARENESS STRATEGIES

Have you ever had a coworker approach you, and without you saying anything, he understood what kind of day you were having and where your mind was wandering? He knew you must have come from a meeting with so-and-so because he could "see it" all over your face. He knew it was probably time to let you vent, instead of asking for that favor he had in mind. He must have picked up on something.

Or how about that waitress who seems to "just know" what each of her customers need: one couple is in their own world and prefers to be alone; another couple welcomes some fresh conversation from a new person, while another table wants professional and polite service, minus the small talk. Everyone is sitting at a table to eat and drink and be served, and yet there is so much below the surface that makes each table unique. How does she quickly size up these tables and know their needs?

Both this perceptive coworker and the waitress have a high level of social awareness—a skill they use to recognize and understand the moods of other individuals and entire groups of people. Though these two may be seasoned veterans at this, it is a skill that they most likely learned and practiced over time.

Instead of looking inward to learn about and understand yourself, social awareness is looking outward to learn about and appreciate others. Social awareness is centered on your ability to recognize and understand the emotions of others. Tuning into others' emotions as you interact with them will help you get a more accurate view of your surroundings, which affects everything from relationships to the bottom line.

To build your social awareness skills, you will find yourself observing people in all kinds of situations. You may be observing someone from afar while you're in a checkout line, or you may be right in the middle of a conversation observing the person to whom you are speaking. You will learn to pick up on body language, facial expressions, postures, tone of voice, and even what is hidden beneath the surface, like deeper emotions and thoughts.

One of the intriguing things about building an acute sense of social awareness is that emotions, facial expressions, and body language have been shown to translate across many different cultures. You can use these skills wherever you are.

The lens you look through must be clear. Making sure you are present and able to give others your full attention is the first step to becoming more socially aware. Looking outward isn't just about using your eyes: it means tapping into your senses. Not only can you fully utilize your basic five senses, but you can also include the vast amount of information coming into your brain through your sixth sense—your emotions. Your emotions can help you notice and interpret cues other people send you. These cues will give you some help in putting yourself in the other person's shoes.

The 17 strategies in this section will help you tackle the obstacles that get in your way and provide you with a helping hand when the going gets tough. You can only attend to so much, so it's critical to pick up on the right signals. These proven social awareness strategies will help you do just that.

Social Awareness Strategies

SOCIAL AWARENESS STRATEGIES

1. Greet People by Name
2. Watch Body Language
3. Make Timing Everything
4. Develop a Back-pocket Question
5. Don't Take Notes at Meetings
6. Plan Ahead for Social Gatherings
7. Clear Away the Clutter
8. Live in the Moment
9. Go on a 15-minute Tour
10. Watch EQ at the Movies
11. Practice the Art of Listening
12. Go People Watching
13. Understand the Rules of the Culture Game
14. Test for Accuracy
15. Step into Their Shoes
16. Seek the Whole Picture
17. Catch the Mood of the Room

1 Greet People by Name

Maybe you've been named after a special relative or family friend, or maybe you have a nickname that abbreviates your long last name. Whatever the story is behind your name, it's an essential part of your identity. It feels so good when people use your name and remember it.

Greeting someone by name is one of the most basic and influential social awareness strategies you can adopt. It's a personal and meaningful way to engage someone. If you have a tendency to withdraw in social situations, greeting someone by name is a simple way to stick your neck out; using someone's name breaks down barriers and comes across as warm and inviting. Even if you are a social butterfly, greeting people by name is a strategy to live by.

> **Whatever the story is behind your name, it's an essential part of your identity. It feels so good when people use your name and remember it.**

Social Awareness Strategies

Enough said about the value of greeting by name. Now let's talk about following through. If names are usually on the tip of your tongue, you claim to be "great with faces, but not names," or you can't seem to remember anyone's name 30 seconds after you hear it—make this the month to practice saying, "Hello,

[name]," to someone each time you enter a room and to those you're introduced to. Remembering a person's name is a brain exercise—practice may be required. If a name sounds unusual to you, ask the person to spell it for you so you can picture the name written. This will help you remember it later. Be sure to use the person's name at least twice during the conversation.

Greeting people by their names not only acknowledges them as the essence of who they are, but also allows you to remain connected to them in more than just a superficial way. By making it a goal to remember someone's name when you meet or greet him or her, you are focusing your mind, which will only increase your awareness in social situations.

2 Watch Body Language

Ask professional poker players what they study most carefully about their opponents, and they will tell you they look for small changes in behavior that indicate a player's confidence in his hand.

They check posture, eye movement, hand gestures, and facial expressions. The confident player with bravado is often the bluff, while the quiet hand is the royal flush waiting to sneak up from behind. For professional poker players, reading body language is a matter of winning or going home empty-handed. Acute social awareness skills literally make or break them.

It's just as important for us to become expert readers of body language; we'll know how people are really feeling and can plan an appropriate response. To get a complete read from a person, do a head-to-toe body language assessment. Start with the head and face. The eyes communicate more than any other part of the human anatomy. You can get a lot of information from them, but be careful not to stare. Maintained eye contact can show if a person is trustworthy, sincere, or caring. Shifty eyes or too much blinking can suggest deception. People whose eye movements are relaxed yet attentive to the person they are conversing with are more sincere and honest.

Next, look at the person's smile. Is it authentic or forced? Researchers can tell the difference. They look for a crinkle of skin in the corner of the eyes, and if it is not there, the smile is probably fake. Authentic smiles change rapidly from a small facial movement to a broad open expression.

Once you've finished with the face, move to the shoulders, torso, and limbs. Are the shoulders slouched or held naturally upright? Are the arms, hands, legs, and feet calm or fidgety? The body communicates nonstop and is an abundant source of information, so purposefully watch body language during meetings, friendly encounters, and first introductions. Once you tune into body language, its messages will become loud and clear, and you'll soon notice cues and be able to call someone's bluff.

3 Make Timing Everything

You've probably heard the phrase "timing is everything" to explain hundreds of situations and scenarios. When dealing with people and their emotions, timing really is everything. You don't ask for a raise when business is not going well, you don't try to correct someone who feels threatened by you, and you don't ask for a favor when someone is under a lot of stress or angry.

To practice your timing as it relates to social awareness, start working on your timing with asking questions. The goal is to ask the right questions at the right time with the right frame of mind, all with your audience in mind.

Just think about how it would go over if you were talking with a colleague who is venting about her spouse. She is concerned about her marriage, and is showing more emotion than ever. As a response, you blurt out the question, "Have you thought about what ideas you have for the project proposal yet?" She stares at you blankly and is blindsided by your question. Her face drops. The conversation is over.

In this case, the timing, the question, and the frame of mind were wrong. You asked the right question at the right time for you; but the time and frame of mind of the other person were way off. Remember, this isn't about you—it's about the other person. An appropriate question at that time for her frame of mind would have been, "Is there anything I can do for you?" Most likely, she would've appreciated your concern, and calmed down. At that point, you could've gently asked your question, most likely acknowledging that the timing was still a little off.

As you practice your timing, remember that the key to social awareness is focusing on others, instead of on yourself, so that you can be more effective.

4 Develop a Back-pocket Question

Sometimes conversations just don't go as planned. Either the other person isn't talking as much as you expected, or you are getting one-word answers. A 10-second chunk of silence feels like an eternity; you cringe because it is so awkward. You need to pull something out of your back pocket fast. How about a handy back-pocket question?

A back-pocket question is what you use *just in case* to bail you out of any awkward silence or uncomfortable moment. This social awareness strategy buys you time so you can get to know someone better and shows the other person that you are interested in his or her thoughts, feelings, and ideas. It can be something like: "What do you think about [fill in blank]?" Pick from a handful of issues that require some explanation like work or current events, but avoid politics, religion, and other potentially sensitive areas.

The versatile conversationalist knows exactly when to pull out his or her back-pocket question—the conversation needs a kick start, and you're just not ready to give up yet. It may feel like an abrupt subject change. Don't worry; if it injects life into the conversation, you've done well. If there's still dead air, it might be time to politely include someone else in the conversation or excuse yourself to refill your beverage.

5 Don't Take Notes at Meetings

It's been hammered into our heads that if we want to be successful, we need to learn to juggle a hectic workload and take on more and more. With multi-tasking, the more you can juggle, the more successful you are, right? Wrong. Multi-tasking actually sacrifices your quality of work, as the brain is simply incapable of performing at a high level in multiple activities at once.

Let's say you're in a meeting where several ideas are being shared. Pros and cons of each idea are tossed about the room. Though the notes are being captured on flipcharts, you prefer to take your own so you don't miss any details. As you finish your last thoughts, suddenly Oscar's voice shifts abruptly from an even tone to one that's clearly annoyed. A terse exchange between Oscar and Melinda ensues. You review your notes and can't find the cause of this shift. What just happened? You missed critical details.

By having your head focused on your tablet and your hand scribbling away, you miss the critical clues that shed some major light on how others are feeling or what they may be thinking. Someone who wants the whole story and complete picture observes others without the distraction of phones, typing, or writing. Instead, he or she simply observes.

Remember, the main goal of social awareness is to recognize and understand how others are thinking and feeling. To do this, you need to focus on other people.

A great place to observe others is at meetings. There's already a captive audience, and usually there's minimal distraction with email and phone—but there's the mighty pen. At your next meeting, don't take notes. Instead, look at each person's face and notice his or her expressions. Make eye contact with whoever is speaking. You will feel more engaged and focused on others, and pick up on things that pen and paper surely miss.

By having your head focused on your tablet and your hand scribbling away, you miss the critical clues that shed some major light on how others are feeling or what they may be thinking.

Note-taking certainly has its value. But it doesn't have to be your modus operandi, either. If you need to take notes for practical purposes, temporarily stop at intervals to practice observation.

6 Plan Ahead for Social Gatherings

Picture yourself leaving a dinner party. You can't believe you forgot to bring the bread. You spent at least 10 minutes at the party beating yourself up over it, and another 15 taking ribbing from your breadless yet good-natured friends. As you put your keys in the ignition, you suddenly remember that you wanted to get Jack's business card to call him about a marketing venture, but the "bread incident" got you off track. Then there's Kate. She seemed down throughout dinner. Why didn't you ask her about it when you were there?

You planned to attend this dinner, but did you plan for it? Planning ahead for an event can be your saving grace, whether the event is a dinner party or a work meeting. If you walk through the door with a plan, you free up your mental energy and brainpower so you can focus on the present moment.

The next time you RSVP for an event, in your next breath remind yourself to plan. On an index card, list who is going to be at the event and list any talking points or to do's. Don't be shy—carry the list with you!

Now let's replay the former party scenario, but this time with your plan on paper and in tow. After you arrive, you give the host that promised loaf of bread. Check. You spot Jack in the kitchen, and move toward him to fit in a quick chat and request that business card. Check. With that done, you notice that Kate is off—she looks somber. You notice right away, not as an afterthought while you drive home. You immediately address the alarm in your brain and pull Kate aside to see if she needs to talk. She appreciates your concern, smiles, and shares her story. With that, you both return to the group and enjoy the meal in front of you.

A bit of planning will not just prepare you for the event; planning will also help you enjoy the event more because you'll be less stressed and more present while you're there.

7 Clear Away the Clutter

To be socially aware, you must be socially present and remove distractions—especially the ones inside your head. These internal distractions are much like clutter in your garage or closet—there's useful stuff in there, but it's crowded and hard to get to what you need. The solution: clear away the clutter.

There are a few culprits that are worthy of spring cleaning. First, we all have conversations and chatter going on inside our heads; we talk to ourselves constantly. We're so busy having these internal chats that we tune the outside world out—which is counterproductive to social awareness. The second culprit is a process where we form our responses while the person we're talking with is still, in fact, talking. This, too, is counterproductive—it's tough to listen to yourself and the other person fully.

To clean up this internal clutter, there are some simple steps to follow. When you are in a conversation, don't interrupt the other person until he or she is completely finished. Next, to squelch the voice that is planning your response, it's important to catch yourself in the act; and when you do, stop yourself and clear away the clutter. Now refocus yourself on the person's face and words. If you need to, physically lean toward the speaker to focus your body into the conversation.

This awareness proves you're making progress because, at one time, you didn't realize this pattern existed.

Remind yourself that you are in the conversation to listen and learn something, not to wow the other person with your insightful remarks. As you continue to be aware of your clutter and clear it, you'll become better at quieting your inner thoughts, and your listening skills will sharpen.

8 Live in the Moment

There's no one better at living in the moment than a child. A child does not think about what happened yesterday or what he's going to do later today. In the moment, he is Superman, and while he is fighting the bad guys, nothing else in the world exists.

Adults, on the other hand, worry about the past (*Oh, I should not have done that*) and stress about the future (*How am I going to handle this tomorrow?*). It's impossible to focus on the present while the future and the past loom. Social awareness requires that you live in the moment as naturally as a child does, so you can notice what's happening with others right now.

> **Remember, planning the future and reflecting on the past are valuable exercises, but doing this throughout your day interferes with what is in front of you— your present.**

Make being in the present moment a habit; it will only lift your social awareness skills. Starting this month, if you are at the gym, then *be* at the gym. If you are at a meeting, *be* at the meeting. Wherever you are, be as present as possible so that you see the people around you and experience life in the moment. If you catch yourself being somewhere else mentally, snap back to the present. Remember, planning the future and reflecting on the past are valuable exercises, but doing this throughout your day interferes with what is in front of you—your present.

9 Go on a 15-minute Tour

Didn't someone say that life is about the journey, not the destination? To become socially aware, we need to remember to enjoy the journey and notice people along the way. When you are focused only on getting to the next meeting, starting your next class period, seeing the next patient, making it to all your client sites, or hurrying to send an email, you're missing all of the people between Points A and B.

To commit some time to the journey, take some time to walk around where you work and notice your surroundings. Going on a short tour will help you get in tune with other people and their emotions, and refocus your attention on some of the smaller yet critical social clues that exist right under your nose.

During any workday, take just 15 minutes to observe things you've never noticed before. Things to look for include the look and feel of people's workspaces, the timing of when different people move around the office, and which people seek interaction versus those who stay at their desks all day.

After your first observation tour, select a different day to tour your workspace for moods. Other people's moods can provide you with critical hints about how things are going both individually and collectively. Notice what people may be feeling or how they make you feel when you drop by to talk briefly. Also observe the overall mood in the office or the school, patient care area, manufacturing floor—whatever your work area looks like. Focus intently on what you see, hear, and pick up on in other people.

Schedule 15 minutes to tour your workplace twice a week for a month. On the days you tour, be sure to avoid making too many assumptions or conclusions—just simply observe. You'll be amazed at what you see along the way.

10 Watch EQ at the Movies

Hollywood. It's the entertainment capital of the world known for glitz, glamour, and celebrity. Believe it or not, Hollywood is also a hotbed of EQ, ripe for building your social awareness skills.

After all, art imitates life, right? Movies are an abundant source of EQ skills in action, demonstrating behaviors to emulate or completely avoid. Great actors are masters at evoking real emotion in themselves; as their characters are scripted to do outrageous and obvious things, it's easy to observe the cues and emotions on-screen.

To build social awareness skills, you need to practice being aware of what's happening with other people; it doesn't matter if you practice using a box office hero or a real person. When you watch a movie to observe social cues, you're practicing social awareness. Plus, since you are not living the situation, you're not emotionally involved, and the distractions are limited. You can use your mental energy to observe the characters instead of dealing with your own life.

This month, make it a point to watch two movies specifically to observe the character interactions, relationships, and conflicts. Look for body language clues to figure out how each character is feeling and observe how the characters handle the conflicts. As more information about the characters unfold, rewind and watch past moments to spot clues you may have missed the first time. Believe it or not, watching movies from the land of make-believe is one of the most useful and entertaining ways to practice your social awareness skills for the real world.

11 Practice the Art of Listening

This sounds basic—almost too basic to mention—but listening is a strategy and a skill that is losing ground in society. Most people think they are good listeners, but if adults played "the Telephone Game" today, how accurate would the final message be? Listening requires focus, and focus isn't easy because we're stretched in several directions.

Listening isn't just about hearing words; it's also about listening to the tone, speed, and volume of the voice. What is being said? Is anything not being said? What hidden messages exist below the surface? You may have sat through a speech or presentation where powerful words were chosen, but the tone, speed, or volume didn't match the power of the words. Instead, these likely matched the speaker's frame of mind.

Here's the strategy to practice: when someone is talking to you, stop everything else and listen fully until the other person is finished speaking. When you are on a phone call, don't type an email. When your son asks you a question, put your laptop down and look at him while you respond. When you're eating dinner with your family, turn off the TV and listen to the conversation around the table. When you're meeting with someone, close the door and sit near the person so you can focus and listen. Simple things like these will help you stay in the present moment, pick up on the cues the other person sends, and really hear what he or she is saying.

12 Go People Watching

Sometimes all you want to do is just sit back and watch the world go by—or, in this case, people. Sit back at a table at your local coffee shop and just observe all the people going in and out with their grande, non-fat, extra-hot lattes or the couples walking hand-in-hand on the street: you are actually engaging in one of the most effective social awareness strategies yet.

When you take the time to observe, you will notice people reveal their moods. Watch how people interact with each other in the line at the local coffee shop, grocery store, or other public places: these are great practice arenas. You will see people looking at shelves in stores, and the pace at which they move. You can keep a safe distance and use this as a trial run in spotting the body language or nonverbal cues to tip you off to what people are feeling or thinking.

People watching is a safe way for you to pick up on signals, observe interactions, and figure out underlying motivations or emotions without entering into the interaction yourself. Being able to identify the moods and emotions of others is a huge part of social awareness, and often, these are things that fly under your radar. So, in the next week, head out to your local coffee shop, grab a beverage that strikes your fancy, and get comfortable—because it's the perfect place to work on social awareness.

13 Understand the Rules of the Culture Game

Social awareness extends beyond just picking up on another person's emotional cues. Let's say you start a new job at a company. To be successful, you will need to learn how things are done in this company's culture. You are assigned to share an office with Lac Su. To be successful with Lac, you'll also need to learn how Lac's cultural and family background influences his expectations of you as an office mate. You can't interpret his actions or reactions until you learn Lac's rules of the game.

Rules? Much of doing and saying the right things in social situations comes from understanding the rules of the culture game. Our world is a melting pot of vastly different cultures. These cultures interact, live, and conduct business with each other according to very specific rules. There is no way around it, and it is a requirement to learn how to become emotionally intelligent across cultures.

The secret to winning this culture game is to treat others how they want to be treated, not how you would want to be treated. The trick is identifying the different rules for each culture. To make matters even more complicated, the rules you should be watching for and mastering include the rules not only of ethnic culture but also of family and business culture.

How do you go about mastering multiple sets of rules at once? The first step is to listen and watch even more and for a longer period of time than you would with people from your own culture. Collect multiple observations and think before you jump to conclusions. Consider yourself new in town, and before you open your mouth and insert your foot, observe other people's interactions. Look for similarities and differences between how you would play the game versus how others are playing it.

Next, ask specific questions. This may require talking in settings outside meetings or on the sidelines. Many cultures, both business and ethnic, value social interaction around meals before getting down to business. There is wisdom in this approach because social interaction raises social awareness for both parties and prepares them for playing by the rules of the game.

14 Test for Accuracy

Even the most socially aware people have off-days or situations they can't quite read. Maybe there's so much interference and activity with people or the room that it's difficult to get a good reading in the midst of the hectic pace. Or perhaps these socially aware people are almost sure they know what's going on but need some validation of their observations. In these cases, there's a social awareness strategy to get the answers you need: just ask.

Just ask? Remember, there's no such thing as a silly question. Whether you're a novice or an expert in social awareness, we all need to confirm social observations at some point. The best way to test your accuracy is to simply ask if what you're observing in people or situations is actually what's occurring.

Maybe you have run into Steve at work and noticed that he has a sullen look on his face, with his head hanging low and his eyes never looking up from the ground. You ask how he is doing, and he says he is doing "just fine."

Your evidence is telling you otherwise—he says he's fine, but he doesn't appear to be fine. In this moment, ask a reflective question to clarify what you are seeing. Say something like, "It looks like you are feeling down about something. Did something happen?" Simply stating what evidence you see (*it looks like you are feeling down*) and asking a direct question (*did something happen?*) is a reflective statement at its best. You will likely hear whatever he wants you to know for now; but you've reached out to Steve and let him know that you are interested.

Another type of question that tests for accuracy focuses on unspoken messages—or what wasn't necessarily said. Since people don't always openly and directly say how they feel about something, they'll drop hints. If you feel comfortable asking, this is a great opportunity to see if you picked up on the hints and what you think they meant. You will also have the opportunity to catch your mistakes if you've jumped to conclusions or missed a cue.

Testing your observations for accuracy will ultimately give you a keener understanding of social situations, and help you pick up on cues that usually fly under the radar. If you don't ask, you'll never be sure.

15 Step into Their Shoes

Actors do this all the time—they walk in characters' shoes for a living. Actors channel the same emotions and feelings, embodying the minds and motivations of the characters. It's how actors with great, healthy upbringings are able to play the most convincing, dysfunctional characters—and vice versa. After actors' work is complete, instead of complaining about the process, they often report that they come to appreciate the characters they inhabit—even if it's the bad guy.

Walking in the shoes of another is social awareness at its best—and it's not just for actors. It's for all of us who want to gain perspective and a deeper understanding of others, improve our communication, and identify problems before they escalate. If you don't think you need this, when was the last time you thought, *I wish I had known that Jane felt that way*. If you're wishing, it's already too late; wouldn't it be more useful to catch Jane sooner in the situation?

To practice this strategy, you need to ask yourself questions that start with, "If I were this person . . . ." Let's say you're in a meeting and someone puts Jim on the spot, questioning decisions he made on a project that had issues. If you were the one who had to answer the question, your tendencies would put you on the defensive. But, remember, this isn't about you—it's now about Jim. Put away your own beliefs, emotions, thinking patterns, and tendencies— it's about experiencing this situation as Jim. Ask yourself, *If I were Jim, how would I respond to this question?* To answer this, use your previous history with Jim to help you understand him: how he's reacted in similar situations in the past, how he deals with being put on the spot, how he handles himself in groups and one-on-one. How did he act, and what did he say? This is all critical information.

How do you know if you're on target? If you're comfortable with Jim and the timing is right, approach him after the meeting and test your thoughts. If you're not comfortable with Jim, practice using another situation with someone else and test your thoughts. The more you practice and get feedback, the more comfortable you'll become in the shoes of others.

16   **Seek the Whole Picture**

Since we see ourselves through our own rose-colored glasses, chances are we're seeing only part of the picture. If you had the opportunity, would you be willing to see yourself through the eyes of those who know you best? Looking outward and seeking this feedback are key to social awareness, because this gives us the chance to see how others view us—to see the whole picture.

Taking advantage of this opportunity requires *courage and strength* to invite your fans, as well as your critics, to get down to the nitty-gritty and honestly share their perceptions of you. What if they're wrong? What if they're harsh? What if they're right?

Regardless of the answers, their perceptions matter because others' opinions of you influence you and your life. For example, if people think you are passive in meetings when you simply need time to think before speaking, their perceptions begin to shape what opportunities are offered to you. Soon your boss is passing you over for chairing a committee because you are perceived as passive instead of thoughtful.

The best method for seeing how others perceive you is simple and powerful. For matters of EQ, you can send a

360-degree survey that asks you and other people questions about your self-awareness, self-management, social awareness, and relationship management skills. The result is a complete picture of your own and others' perceptions. Believe it or not, what others say about you is usually more accurate than what you think about yourself. Nonetheless, whatever these perceptions are, becoming aware is important so you know how they will shape you.

Muster some of that strength and gather other people to help you out in understanding yourself a bit more through their eyes. Other than becoming a fly on the wall or videotaping yourself, this is what it takes to see yourself in action through the eyes of others.

17 Catch the Mood of the Room

Once you've mastered reading the cues and emotions of other people, you're ready to read an entire room. It may sound daunting, but it's what you've already learned about social awareness—just on a larger scale.

Essentially, there are two ways to pick up the mood of an entire room. First, you can rely solely on your gut instincts.

> **Emotions are contagious, meaning they spread from one or two people until there's a palpable and collective mood that you will feel at some level.**

Emotions are contagious, meaning they spread from one or two people until there's a palpable and collective mood that you will feel at some level. For example, imagine walking into a room of 125 entrepreneurs who are networking and sharing their ideas. It's pretty likely that there would be excitement and positive energy there, and it wouldn't take long to become aware of it. You'd hear their voice levels and tones, and see the focused and interested posture and body language. Now imagine walking into a room of 125 people waiting to be chosen for jury duty. The room is quiet; people are trying to distract themselves with reading material, music, and anything else to pass the time. Even though it's our civic duty to attend, hardly anyone wants to be there. The two moods are like night and day.

Here's how you can catch the mood of the room. When you enter the room, scan it and notice whether you feel and see energy or quiet, subdued calm. Take notice of how people are arranging themselves—alone or in groups. Are they talking and moving their hands? Are some more animated than others? What is your gut telling you about them?

Another way to read the mood of the room is to bring along a more experienced guide, much like you would on an African safari. Your guide should be a socially aware expert willing to show you the ropes when it comes to tapping into your instincts and picking up the room's mood. Shadow your guide and listen to what he feels and sees. Ask what he senses and what clues gave the mood away. Eventually, you should be the one to take the lead. Size up the room, and share and compare your thoughts with your guide. Through this exercise, you will soon pick up on observations like your guide does, in time doing so on your own.

Human nature and behavior may not be that far from what happens on the open African savannah. The sooner you can hone your ability to spot safety, concern, or shifts in moods in group settings, the more skilled you will be in maneuvering through the social wilds of your life.

8

RELATIONSHIP MANAGEMENT STRATEGIES

Most people have a spring in their step and put their best foot forward when they are in a new relationship (work or otherwise), but they stumble and lose their footing trying to maintain relationships over the long term. Reality soon sets in that the honeymoon phase is officially over.

The truth is, all relationships take work, even the great ones that seem effortless. We've all heard this, but do we really *get* it?

Working on a relationship takes time, effort, and know-how. The know-how is emotional intelligence. If you want a relationship that has staying power and grows over time, and in which your needs and the other person's needs are satisfied, the final EQ skill—relationship management—is just what the doctor ordered.

Thankfully, these relationship management skills can be learned, and they tap into the three other EQ skills that you're familiar with—self-awareness, self-management, and social awareness. You use your self-awareness skills to notice your feelings and judge if your needs are being satisfied. You use your self-management skills to express your feelings and act accordingly to benefit the connection. Finally, you use your social awareness skills to better understand the other person's needs and feelings.

In the end, no man is an island; relationships are an essential and fulfilling part of life. Since you are half of any relationship, you have half of the responsibility of deepening these connections. The following 17 strategies will help you work on what's critical to making relationships work.

RELATIONSHIP MANAGEMENT STRATEGIES

1.   Be Open and Be Curious
2.   Enhance Your Natural Communication Style
3.   Avoid Giving Mixed Signals
4.   Remember the Little Things That Pack a Punch
5.   Take Feedback Well
6.   Build Trust
7.   Have an "Open-door" Policy
8.   Only Get Mad on Purpose
9.   Don't Avoid the Inevitable
10. Acknowledge the Other Person's Feelings
11. Complement the Person's Emotions or Situation
12. When You Care, Show It
13. Explain Your Decisions, Don't Just Make Them
14. Make Your Feedback Direct and Constructive
15. Align Your *Intention* with Your *Impact*
16. Offer a "Fix-it" Statement during a Broken Conversation
17. Tackle a Tough Conversation

1 Be Open and Be Curious

We can imagine a few readers thinking, "Oh brother, I have to be open and curious with people at work? Can I just work on my projects and what I was hired to do, minus the touchy-feely stuff?" Actually, establishing, building, and maintaining relationships are all part of your job—even if you work with just one other person. Maintaining relationships may not be on your job description and may not have even been discussed, but for you to be successful, being open and curious is absolutely, unequivocally part of your job.

Let's explore what "open" means in terms of relationship management. Being open means sharing information about yourself with others. You can use your self-management skills to choose how open you are and what you share, but know that there's a benefit to opening up that may help you with your choices: when people know about you, there's less room for them to misinterpret you. For example, if you are particularly sensitive about showing up five minutes early to meetings, and get annoyed when people stroll in at the very beginning of the meeting or even a little late, some people might interpret you as being uptight and rigid. If you shared with these same people that you were in the Marines for the first years of your career, your coworkers would understand and maybe even appreciate your sense of timing and courtesy. Who knows, your punctuality might even rub off!

Being an open book on your end isn't the whole story with managing a relationship—you also need to be interested in the other person's story as well. In other words, you need to be curious. The more you show interest in and learn about the other person, the better shot you have at meeting his or her needs and not misinterpreting them.

When you ask questions, draw from your social awareness skills to choose an appropriate setting and time. Be inquisitive in your tone—similar to how Santa Claus asks a child what he'd like for Christmas. The opposite tone is judgmental—think of someone who's ever asked you a question like, "Why on earth did you buy a motorcycle?" or "You majored in philosophy? What did you plan to do with THAT?"

When you ask questions and this person opens up, you will not only learn information that will help you manage the relationship, but the other person will also appreciate the interest shown in him or her. If you are beginning a new relationship, in an established one, or even if you're in a rough patch, take a few minutes out of your day to identify a few relationships that need some attention, and make time to be open and curious with these people.

2 Enhance Your Natural Communication Style

Whether it's putting your two cents in when others are talking to you or shying away from a disagreement, your natural communication style shapes your relationships. Now you have the opportunity to use your self-awareness, self-management, and social awareness skills to shape your natural style.

At the top of a page in a journal, describe what your natural style is. You can call it whatever you would like. Think about how your friends, family, and colleagues experience your style. Is it direct, indirect, comfortable, serious, entertaining, discreet, controlled, chatty, intense, curious, cool, intrusive? You name it because you've likely heard about it more than once.

On the left side of the paper, jot down the upsides of your natural style. These are the things people appreciate about how you interact with them. On the right side, list the downsides or things that have created confusion, weird reactions, or trouble.

Once your list is complete, choose three upsides that you can use more to improve your communication. Next, choose three downsides, and think about ways you can either eliminate, downplay, or improve them. Be honest with yourself about what you will or won't do. If you need help figuring out what will give you the biggest results, just ask your friends, coworkers, and family for their suggestions. Making your plan public will also build in accountability that can help you make a lasting improvement in your relationships.

3 Avoid Giving Mixed Signals

We all rely on stoplights to safely direct us through intersections dozens of times each week. When the stoplights aren't working, and the lights either blink to proceed with caution or are out altogether, the intersection transforms into an every-man-for-himself situation. People are confused; and when it's their turn to cross, they gingerly look all ways before moving ahead. With functioning stoplights, we have confidence in the system because it's clear what we do—stop on red, and go on green. It's the same for signals that we send to the people in our relationships.

Feelings express truth, and they have a way of rising to the surface through our reactions and body language, despite the words we choose. Telling your staff in a muted voice and frowning face that they did a great job on the product launch doesn't match up; the words and the body language are mixed. People trust what they see over what they hear.

Even if you're a good self-manager, your emotions rise to the surface. You experience many emotions every day, and your brain can't sort through every single one. When you talk with someone, you may be saying one thing that's on your mind as your body reacts to an emotion you experienced minutes ago.

You confuse and frustrate others when you say one thing and your body or tone say another. Over time, this confusion will cause communication issues that will affect your relationships. To resolve the mixed signal issue, use your self-awareness skills to identify your emotions, and use yourself-management

People trust what they see over what they hear.

skills to decide which feelings to express and how to express them.

Sometimes it might not be appropriate to match your signals. Let's say you become angry in a meeting and can't really show your emotion at that moment. Just put your anger on the back burner for the moment, but don't disregard the feeling forever. Choose a time when you can express your anger: when it doesn't work against you but instead produces the most positive results. If your emotion is strong enough and you can't put off expressing it, your best bet is to explain what's happening (i.e., "If I seem distracted, it's because I can't stop worrying about a phone call that went awry this morning").

For the next month, pay close attention to matching your tone and body language to what you are really trying to say. Take mental note of those moments when you tell someone that you are feeling fine, but your body, tone, or demeanor is sending drastically different signals. When you catch yourself sending a mixed signal, readjust to match it or explain it.

Relationship Management Strategies

4 Remember the Little Things That Pack a Punch

It's pretty obvious on any news channel, reality show, sitcom, or newspaper that today's media feed off the idea that courtesy appears to be diminishing in modern society. With the decline of good manners, there are fewer expressions of appreciation. These days, in both personal and work-related relationships, there are far too few "please's," "thank you's," and "I'm sorry's" being expressed.

Most workers will say that they *never* get thanked for their contributions at work but yet will agree that hearing "thank you," "please," or even "I'm sorry" can have a positive impact on morale.

Think about how often you really say "thank you," "please," or "I'm sorry" when it is needed; if you don't use them often, it could be due to lack of time or habit, or maybe even a bruised ego. Begin to make a habit of incorporating more of these phrases into your relationships. Or, rather, please make it a habit to use more of these phrases during your day. Thank you.

5 Take Feedback Well

Feedback is a unique gift. It's meant to help us improve in ways that we perhaps cannot see on our own. Since you never know exactly what you are going to receive, however, feedback is sometimes like opening up a present and looking inside to find a pair of tiger-striped socks with red sequins.

The element of surprise can catch us off guard, so we need to use our self-awareness skills to prepare ourselves for that moment. *What do I feel when I am on the spot and surprised? How do I show it?* With that awareness, move on to your self-management skills: *what response should I choose?*

To help you receive feedback well, let's break it down. First, consider the source of your feedback. This person probably has a relevant perspective—he or she knows you and has seen your performance—and has an interest in seeing you improve.

As you receive feedback, turn on your social awareness skills to listen and really hear what is being said. Ask clarifying questions and ask for examples to better understand the person's perspective. Whether you agree with what was said or not, thank the person for his or her willingness to share, because it takes almost as much grace to give feedback as it does to receive it.

After you receive the feedback, use your self-management skills to decide your next steps; don't feel pressured to rush into action. Time can help you absorb the underlying point, sort out your feelings and thoughts, and help you to decide what to do about the feedback. Remember the Emotion vs. Reason list?

Receiving feedback is probably the hardest part of the process. Once you decide what to do with the feedback, follow up with plans. Actually making adjustments will show the person who gave you feedback that you value his or her comments. Take the person's feedback seriously and try what he or she suggested. There may be no better way to solidify your relationship with him or her.

6 Build Trust

Have you ever been asked to "practice" trust? The exercise looks like this: you have a partner, and you stand about five feet in front of the person with your back facing him. You close your eyes, and on a count of three, you fall backward toward the person so that he can catch you. When you're caught, everyone enjoys a laugh and is thankful neither person wiped out. If only trust were a matter of good, strong arms and steady balance.

An unknown author said, "Trust is a peculiar resource; it is built rather than depleted by use." Trust is something that takes time to build, can be lost in seconds, and may be our most important and most difficult objective in managing our relationships.

> **Trust is a peculiar resource; it is built rather than depleted by use.**

How is trust built? Open communication; willingness to share; consistency in words, actions, and behavior over time; and reliability in following through on the agreements of the relationship, just to name a few examples. It's ironic that, for most relationships, a certain level of trust needs to be present in order for you to develop trust.

To build trust, use your self-awareness and self-management skills to be the first to lay some of yourself on the line and share something about you. Remember, you should share parts of yourself at a time; don't feel like you have to be a complete open book up front.

To manage your relationships, you need to manage your trust of others, and their trust level of you is critical to deepening your connection with others. Cultivating relationships and building trust take time. Identify the relationships in your life that need more trust, and use your self-awareness skills to ask yourself what is missing. Use your social awareness skills to ask the other person what needs to happen to build trust—and listen to the answer. Asking will show you care about the relationship, which will help to build trust, and deepen the relationship.

7 Have an "Open-door" Policy

Here's a quick history lesson that you may remember: the Open Door policy originated in 1899 when the United States feared it would lose its trading privileges in the East. The United States declared an "open-door policy," allowing all trading nations access to the Chinese market.

Access: it's an important word that sums up the open-door concept. Access has moved swiftly beyond trading agreements and into the workplace. Today, a true open-door policy allows any employee to talk to anyone at any level, fostering upward communication through direct and easy access to everyone below.

Ask those around you if you should adopt an open-door policy to better manage your relationships. If you need to be more accessible and show people they can have unscheduled, informal conversations with you, then adopting this policy might be right up your alley.

Keep in mind you don't have to stretch yourself too thin by being there for everyone at anytime; you simply have to communicate your policy and then stick to it. Use your self-awareness skills to identify how the policy works for you, and manage yourself to make it work. Ongoing observations

Relationship Management Strategies

of others, also known as social awareness, should help you determine how it's working, too.

Remember, increasing your accessibility can only improve your relationships—it literally opens the door to communication, even if it's virtual (by email or phone). People will feel valued and respected because of the time you're giving them; and you get the opportunity to learn about others. At the end of the day, the policy's a win for you and a win for others.

8 Only Get Mad on Purpose

"Anyone can become angry—that is easy. But to be angry with the right person, to the right degree, at the right time, for the right purpose, and in the right way, this is not easy."

We can thank Greek philosopher Aristotle for those words and enduring insight into managing our emotions and relationships. If you can master this one, consider your EQ journey a success. Anger is an emotion that exists for a reason—anger is not an emotion to stifle or ignore. If you manage it properly and use it purposefully, you can get results that enhance your relationships. Really.

Think of the football coach who gets straight to the point at halftime. His stern feedback grabs his players' attention and focuses them for the second half. The team returns refreshed, refocused, and ready to win; in this case, the coach managed his emotions to motivate others to action. Expressing anger in appropriate ways communicates your strong feelings and reminds people of the gravity of a situation. Expressing anger too much or at the wrong times desensitizes people to what you are feeling, making it hard for others to take you seriously.

Using a strong emotion like anger to benefit your relationships will take time to master, because hopefully you don't have daily opportunities to practice. There's a lot of behind-the-scenes preparation for this strategy, starting with becoming aware of your anger.

Use your self-awareness skills to think about and define your varying degrees of anger—from what annoys you a little to what sends you off the deep end. Write these down and choose words that are specific and then write examples to explain when you feel this way. Determine when you should show your anger based on the criterion that if it's shared it will actually improve the relationship somehow. To make your choices, use your social awareness skills to think about the other people involved and their responses.

Remember, relationship management is about making choices and acting with the goal of creating an honest, deep connection with others. To do this, you need to be honest with others and with yourself, which sometimes means using anger with a purpose.

9 Don't Avoid the Inevitable

You and Marge work in the same shipping and receiving department. She gets under your skin; if you could press a button to ship her to another department, it would've been done five years ago. The problem is, no such button exists, and there's no chance of change. To add fuel to the fire, your boss has just given you and Marge a large project to work on together. She suggests meeting for lunch to talk about the next steps, and you generate a fast list of reasons why you can't make it. You have officially brushed Marge off. Now what? You're still at square one (that's what), and you still have the project and have to figure out how to work together.

This is when relationship management skills are absolutely necessary, because though you might not choose a friendship with this person, you and Marge are now responsible for the same project. Here's a basic strategy to work with Marge: do not avoid her or the situation. Accept it and make the choice to use your EQ skills to move forward with her.

You'll need to watch your emotions, and make decisions about how to manage those emotions. Since you're not in this alone, conjure up your social awareness skills to bring Marge into the fold and put yourself in her shoes. Meet with her to learn about what experience she has to offer and her preferences for working with you on this project. Observe her body language to see how she responds to you; maybe you frustrate her just as much! This may hurt a little, but you may actually lay the groundwork for a working relationship.

Next, share your preferences for managing the project and come to an agreement. You won't need to tell Marge you don't care for her—instead, you can share that you'd prefer to work independently on separate parts of the project and meet along the way to ensure you're both on track. If Marge agrees, your work process has been hammered out. If she doesn't agree, it's time to apply more self-management and social awareness skills until you reach an agreement.

If you get frustrated along the way (and chances are you will), ask yourself why and decide how to manage yourself. Loop back with Marge at your next meeting, and remind yourselves about the goal of the project. At the end of the project, find a way to acknowledge what you both accomplished together.

10 Acknowledge the Other Person's Feelings

If you're known for being terrible with relationships, then this EQ strategy may be a great place to start getting better. Let's say that, one morning, you're pulling into your company's parking lot, and you see your coworker Jessie holding back tears as she exits her car next to you. You ask her if she's OK, and she's not. You respond with, "Well, work will get it off your mind. See you inside." Then you wonder why she avoids you for the rest of the day.

One key to managing relationships is leaning into your own discomfort and taking a moment to acknowledge, not stifle or change, other people's feelings. "I'm sorry you're upset; what can I do?" shows Jessie that if crying is what's going to help her, then you'd be willing to find her a tissue. Simple acts like this one acknowledge emotions without making them a big deal, marginalizing them, or dismissing them. Everyone has a right to experience feelings, even if you might not feel the same way. You don't have to agree with the way people are feeling, but you do have to recognize those feelings as legitimate and respect them.

To help you validate someone's feelings, let's use Jessie's example. Using your social awareness skills, listen to her

Relationship Management Strategies

intently and summarize what you've heard back to her. Not only does it show great listening skills, but it also shows that you're adept at relationship management because you reached out to show you cared, and took an interest in her. You'll end up with a better connection with a now-calm Jessie—and all it took was some time to pay attention and notice her feelings.

11 Complement the Person's Emotions or Situation

If you calmly phone your utility company to have an incorrect fee removed from your monthly bill, you would assume that the customer service representative would be helpful, friendly, and courteous with your request.

Let's say you make the same phone call, but this time you're in a terrible mood. You're feeling testy, agitated, and annoyed at the error. You've been on hold for 10 minutes, which doesn't help. When the customer service rep talks to you, he can hear it in your voice. When he speaks, he sounds serious, as if he wants to resolve this quickly. You appreciate the professionalism and service, check this problem off your list, and move on. This customer service rep is skilled at picking up on cues and adapting to them to give fast, hassle-free service—which benefits the customer and the company as well. And his high EQ makes him promotable and marketable.

What he did exactly is a strategy in relationship management that requires social awareness skills—listening, being present, putting yourself in the shoes of the other person, identifying where someone is emotionally, and choosing an appropriate and complementary response. This last piece, choosing a complementary response, doesn't require you to match or mirror emotions; it wouldn't make sense for the customer service rep to use the same impatient approach you did—that would infuriate you as the customer. Mirroring emotions would also make coworkers and friends recoil. The complementary response always says you recognize what the other person feels and you think it's important.

To practice complementing emotions in your relationships, think about one or two emotional situations you've experienced where there wasn't a lot of gray area and there was at least one other person present. How did the other person respond to you? Did his or her response help or hurt your mood? Was the person able to complement your emotional state? Once you can answer these questions, it's your turn to focus on complementing other people's emotions in the situations they face. Give yourself a week or two to be at the ready for the people in your closest relationships—the people at work or home. Tell yourself your role is to notice their moods and to be there for your coworkers and family members in a helpful way. Whether you are excited or concerned for them, you will show that you are sensitive and care about what they are going through.

12 When You Care, Show It

Here's a true story for aspiring high-EQ managers across the globe. One morning, I groggily went up in the elevator of my office building to start yet another day. It had been a long night the day before; I had stayed late so I could finish some projects for my boss. When I got to my cubicle, I saw that there was a fresh black-and-white cookie and a card that said, "Thanks for filling in the black and whites." It was from my boss. She was always such a busy person, juggling home and work. I was floored to see that she had found a few minutes to slip into a bakery on behalf of my sweet tooth, and get into the office early to put a cookie on my chair. I just about cried at her thoughtfulness.

Talk about the simple things that go a long way. That cookie motivated me to work even harder, and I did so happily and with fierce loyalty.

We hear this story in many forms, but the strategy is always the same. There are people who do great work around you every day. When you care, show it. Don't hesitate or put it off until next week. Do something this week or even today. Things as simple as a greeting card or something else inexpensive, yet meaningful, that sums up how you feel are all you need to make an impact and strengthen a relationship.

13 Explain Your Decisions, Don't Just Make Them

It's frightening to be in a place you're not familiar with and be completely in the dark. Case in point—have you ever planned to go camping but got to the site in the dark? It's hard to get your bearings, you're setting up a tent in the dark, and because you're in the wilderness, it's just eerily quiet and black. You go to bed with one eye open and hope for the best.

The next day, you wake up tired and unzip your tent, and you're amazed at the beauty around you: water, mountains, tree-lined trails, and cute little animals abound. There's nothing to be afraid of—you soon forget last night's anxieties, and you move about your day. What were you so worried about, anyway?

The only difference between these two scenarios is light—it's the same place, and you're with the same people with the same gear. This is what people experience when decisions are made for them. When you are in the dark, intentionally or not, about upcoming layoffs, contract negotiations, and the like, you may as well be setting up camp in blackness. If there are layoffs that increase your workload or change your shift, you'll find out when the pink slips are handed out. If taxes are changed, you'll see it on your paycheck. No recourse, no trial period. It's a done deal.

That's a tough pill to swallow because we're not children or dependents; we're adults. To support an idea, we need to understand *why* the decision was made.

When you use your EQ to manage relationships, keep this in mind. Instead of making a change and expecting others to just accept it, take time to explain the *why* behind the decision, including alternatives, and why the final choice made the most sense. If you can ask for ideas and input ahead of time, it's even better. Finally, acknowledge how the decision will affect everyone. People appreciate this transparency and openness, even though the decision may negatively impact them. Transparency and openness also make people feel like they are trusted, respected, and connected to their organization—instead of being told what to do and kept in the dark.

If you have a habit of making decisions quickly and independently, you're likely very personally competent. Though old habits die hard, since they're ingrained in your brain's wiring, it's time to rewire and add social competence to your decision-making repertoire.

First, you'll likely have to spot your upcoming decisions. Take out your calendar to look over the next three months to identify which decisions will need to be made by then. Now work backward and see who will be impacted by these decisions. Make a complete list of who will be affected by each decision and plan on when and where you will talk together about each, including the details that explain *why* and *how* each decision will be made. If you have to invite people to a special meeting for just this purpose, so be it. As you plan your agenda and your words, use your social awareness skills to put yourself in the shoes of others, so you can speak to your audience before and after you make the decision as they would expect and hope.

14 Make Your Feedback Direct and Constructive

Think about the best feedback you ever received. It wasn't something you necessarily wanted or expected, but it made a difference in your behavior going forward. The feedback may have shaped your overall performance, or how you deal with a particular situation, or even your career. What made the feedback so good?

If you are responsible for giving feedback, there are several guidebooks to walk you through the process, making sure it's within legal and human resources guidelines. Sit down, we have some news: following legal guidelines isn't what makes feedback a performance or person-changing experience; infusing EQ know-how into your feedback, though, is what does.

Here's how to think about feedback and EQ—giving feedback is a relationship-building event that requires all four EQ skills to be effective. Use your self-awareness skills to identify your feelings about the feedback. Are you comfortable with the process? Why or why not? Next, use your self-management skills to

> **Giving feedback is a relationship-building event that requires all four EQ skills to be effective.**

decide what you'll do with the information you just learned about yourself from answering the above questions. For example, if you're anxious about giving feedback about phone etiquette because you don't want people to think you're eavesdropping, how exactly are you going to get beyond this anxiety to confidently give feedback? It's up to you, but don't ignore the feedback because of your discomfort.

Next, use your social awareness skills to think of the person who's receiving the feedback. Remember, feedback is meant to address the problem, not the person. How does the person need to hear your message so it's clear, direct, constructive, and respectful? Constructive feedback has two parts: sharing your opinion and offering solutions for change. Let's take Todd: he's very direct—sugarcoating his need to make phone etiquette improvements will insult him. But if sugarcoating hard news is in his improvement plan, consider sharing feedback with and without the sugar so he can hear the difference and learn from it.

Jenni, on the other hand, is sensitive. Since this is a relationship-building experience, keep Jenni in mind when planning her feedback. Using softeners such as "I think," or "I believe," or "This time" to begin a statement may soften the blow. Instead of "Your report is terrible," use "I believe there are parts of your report that could use revisions. May I walk you through some suggestions?" Here, offering suggestions for improvement is helpful—not prescriptive. At the end, ask the person for his or her thoughts, and thank the person for his or her willingness to consider your suggestions.

15 Align Your *Intention* with Your *Impact*

Let's say you're in a staff meeting and the next topic on the agenda is to figure out why some key deadlines are being missed. After some back-and-forth, it's looking like Ana might be partially to blame—and the room is getting tense. In an honest attempt to lighten the mood, you say something like, "Geez, Ana—looks like maybe taking those longer lunches is finally catching up to you!"

Instead of laughs, there's dead silence. You don't understand what you did wrong, and you later tell Ana, "I was only kidding," but she seems put off. These are the famous last words of someone who had good *intentions*, but the result, or *impact*, was not aligned. And it's too late.

Or think about the results-driven manager who has good intentions about guiding her staff toward achieving higher goals. She's so focused on success that she becomes entrenched in the work (doing most of it herself or pushing everyone to do it her way)—completely missing how to manage the work through others. Her staff deems her a hard-driving micromanager who doesn't share knowledge, and all she *intended* was for the team to learn from her and be successful. Yet again, intentions were good, but they had the opposite impact.

Relationships are now tarnished, and the manager can't figure out why her staff resents her.

If you find that you spend time smoothing things over to repair a relationship, or you are unsure about what's going wrong in your relationships, know that these situations are avoidable. With the help of your awareness and management skills, making small adjustments will make all the difference.

To align your words and actions with your intent, you need to use your social awareness and self-management skills to observe the situation and the people in it, think before you speak or act, and make an appropriate and sensitive response. Do a quick analysis. Think of a situation where the impact of what you said or did was not what you intended. On a piece of paper, describe the incident, your intentions, your actions, and the impact—the end result or reaction of others. Next, write what you didn't realize in the situation—and fill in what you understand now in hindsight, including missed cues, what you learned about yourself, and others. Finally, answer what you could have done differently to keep your intent and impact aligned. If you're not sure, ask someone who was involved in the situation.

In Ana's case, you didn't realize it was the wrong moment for that joke. It singled her out publicly. Next time, you'll lighten the mood by poking fun at yourself, not someone else. The results-driven manager didn't realize what motivated her staff members. She didn't give them space and time to learn and grow on their own. To better manage your relationships, it's critical to spot misalignments before you act, so that your actions match your impact with your good intentions.

16 Offer a "Fix-it" Statement during a Broken Conversation

Airline agents. They are often the bearer of unavoidably bad news in person—weather delays, delays due to mechanical repairs, lost luggage, overbooking. The list goes on and on. Airline agents attempt to repair your broken experience with fix-its or tools—like rebooking and vouchers—to problem solve and address the ultimate goal to get you to your destination.

It's probably safe to assume that we've all had conversations where we could use a fix-it. A simple discussion breaks into a disagreement or gets stuck going around in circles. In these broken conversations, past mistakes may get brought to the surface, regretful comments are made, and blame is present. No matter who said what, or who "started it," it's time to refocus and fix it. Someone needs to step back, quickly assess the situation, and begin repairing the conversation with a fix-it.

To do this, you need to let go of blame and focus on the repair. Do you want to be right, or do you want a resolution? Use your self-awareness skills to see what you are contributing to the situation; self-manage to put your tendencies aside and choose the high road. Your social awareness skills can help you identify what the other person brought to the table or feels. Looking at both sides will help you figure out where the interaction broke down, and which "fix-it" statement is needed to begin the repairs. Fix-it statements feel like a breath of fresh air, are neutral in tone, and find common ground. A "fix-it" statement can be as simple as saying, "This is hard," or asking how the person is feeling. Most conversations can benefit from a fix-it, and it won't do any harm if you feel the conversation breaking down.

> **Fix-it statements feel like a breath of fresh air, are neutral in tone, and find common ground.**

This strategy will help you maintain open lines of communication when you're upset, and with conscious effort and practice, you will be able to fix your broken conversations before they become damaged beyond repair.

17 Tackle a Tough Conversation

"Why did I get passed over for the promotion?" your staff member Judith asks with a slightly defensive tone, a wounded posture, and a quivering voice. This is going to be a tough one. The news leaked out early about Roger's promotion before you could speak with Judith. You value Judith and her work, but you'll need to explain that she's not ready for the next level yet. That's not the hardest part of this conversation—damage control is another story.

From the boardroom to the break room, tough conversations will surface, and it is possible to calmly and effectively handle them. Tough conversations are inevitable; forget running from them because they're sure to catch up to you. Though EQ skills can't make these conversations disappear, acquiring some new skills can make these conversations a lot easier to navigate without ruining the relationship.

1. **Start with agreement.** If you know you are likely to end up in a disagreement, start your discussion with the common ground you share. Whether it's simply agreeing that the discussion will be hard but important or agreeing on a shared goal, create a feeling of agreement. For example: "Judith, I

first want you to know that I value you, and I'm sorry that you learned the news from someone other than me. I'd like to use this time to explain the situation, and anything else you'd like to hear from me. I'd also like to hear from you."

2. **Ask the person to help you understand his or her side.** People want to be heard—if they don't feel heard, frustration rises. Before frustration enters the picture, beat it to the punch and ask the person to share his or her point of view. Manage your own feelings as needed, but focus on understanding the other person's view. In Judith's case, this would sound like, "Judith, along the way I want to make sure you feel comfortable sharing what's on your mind with me. I'd like to make sure I understand your perspective." By asking for Judith's input, you are showing that you care and have an interest in learning more about her. This is an opportunity to deepen and manage your relationship with Judith.

3. **Resist the urge to plan a "comeback" or a rebuttal.** Your brain cannot listen well and prepare to speak at the same time. Use your self-management skills to silence your inner voice and direct your attention to the person in front of you. In this case, Judith has been passed up for a promotion that she was really interested in, and found out about it through the grapevine. Let's face it—if you'd like to maintain the

relationship, you need to be quiet, listen to her shock and disappointment, and resist the urge to defend yourself.

4. **Help the other person understand your side, too.** Now it is your turn to help the other person understand your perspective. Describe your discomfort, your thoughts, your ideas, and the reasons behind your thought process. Communicate clearly and simply; don't speak in circles or in code. In Judith's case, what you say can ultimately be great feedback for her, which she deserves. To explain that Roger had more experience and was more suited for the job at this time is an appropriate message. Since his promotion was leaked to her in an unsavory way, this is something that requires an apology. This ability to explain your thoughts and directly address others in a compassionate way during a difficult situation is a key aspect of relationship management.

5. **Move the conversation forward.** Once you understand each other's perspective, even if there's disagreement, someone has to move things along. In the case of Judith, it's you. Try to find some common ground again. When you're talking to Judith, say something like, "Well, I'm so glad you came to me directly and that we had the opportunity to talk about it. I understand your position, and it sounds like you understand mine. I'm still invested in

your development and would like to work with you on getting the experience you need. What are your thoughts?"

6. **Keep in touch.** The resolution to a tough conversation needs more attention even *after* you leave it, so check progress frequently, ask the other person if he or she is satisfied, and keep in touch as you move forward. You are half of what it takes to keep a relationship oiled and running smoothly. In regard to Judith, meeting with her regularly to talk about her career advancement and promotion potential would continue to show her that you care about her progress.

In the end, when you enter a tough conversation, prepare yourself to take the high road, not be defensive, and remain open by practicing the strategies above. Instead of losing ground with someone in a conversation like this, it can actually become a moment that solidifies your relationship going forward.

EPILOGUE

JUST THE FACTS: A LOOK AT THE LATEST DISCOVERIES IN EMOTIONAL INTELLIGENCE

When TalentSmartEQ® released the *Emotional Intelligence Appraisal®* in 2003, the concept of EQ was still taking root in the minds of business leaders, other professionals, and anyone who simply wanted to lead a happier and healthier life. By measuring people's EQ skills and showing them how to improve in one swoop, the *Emotional Intelligence Appraisal®* quickly became the vehicle that enabled people to turn their newfound emotional mastery into strengthened relationships, better decisions, stronger leadership, and, ultimately, more successful organizations. At TalentSmartEQ®, we've watched more than two million people from the top to the bottom of organizations take the journey to higher EQ.

The field of EQ skill development has truly blossomed since then, and we've taken a special interest in tracking the changing landscape all along the way. The revelations we find in the body of EQ research as well as the insights revealed in our own data often surprise us and encourage us. What remains constant throughout our discoveries is the vitally important role EQ skills play in the quest to lead a happy, healthy, and productive personal and professional life. All offer hope for those looking to increase their EQ skills.

We learn from you, our readers, that you are most interested in the latest trends. As time marches quickly, we invite you to continue reading for a high-level summary of the most robust EQ findings so far and to stay in touch with us for ongoing updates. What follows are highlights from published EQ research since 1995 and from TalentSmartEQ's data trends since 2009 when we first released *Emotional Intelligence 2.0*. To access our previous findings, additional findings, and to learn more about ongoing trends for specific demographic groups, professions, industries, and other interesting topics, please visit our website at www.talentsmarteq.com/eqtrends.

To access ongoing trends, previous findings, and other interesting topics, visit our website at talentsmarteq. com/eqtrends.

Here's what we understand now…

Moods Matter: Emotions Are Catchy

There is still the widespread notion that there's no place for emotions at work. Look up "descriptions of positive work cultures," and you will notice that there is no mention of people being encouraged to constructively express or talk about their emotions. Feeling respected is often mentioned, but the role emotions play in achieving a feeling of respect is not well understood or discussed.

An important and repeatable finding in EQ research shows that emotions in the workplace are contagious. A lack of awareness about this can lead to negative emotions spreading among people working together and interacting with each other. At work, school, and at home, understanding and constructively managing your moods matters because your moods affect those around you. And vice versa. The moods of your coworkers, classmates, and family affect how you feel for the rest of the day too.

Even more notable in the research is the contagion spreading from a specific group to another—leaders to followers. A leader's emotions have been found to be experienced more deeply by followers than by peers. Over time, employees remember more negative emotional displays from their leaders and more intensely. This is not surprising when you consider that supervisors hold power over the people they supervise and their schedules, pay increases, workloads, and work status. When a person's livelihood and professional growth opportunities are at stake, it makes more sense that followers are attuned to the emotions their leaders radiate. An employee's ability to read the boss's mood tells them when they can relax and when they need to be on alert.

The most important conclusion is for leaders. Leaders do not have the luxury of walking through the halls discharging a bad mood. Staff are watching, listening, and feeling their every move. Every leader is responsible for becoming more aware of their moods and which ones should not be spread around the workplace. When leaders want to vent or stew like the rest of us, they need to do so with intention, letting people know. Don't make the mistake of creating needless distraction among your staff. Say at the team meeting, *"If you've seen me in a funk the last two days, it's because I'm sorting out schedules that don't line up, and it's not my favorite thing to do."* You may not hear it, but a wave of relief will rush through the staff's hearts and minds, and they will get back to focusing on the work instead of absorbing or worrying about your bad mood.

> **Every leader is responsible for becoming more aware of their moods and which ones should not be spread around the workplace.**

There is also good news about emotional contagion. Emotional intelligence skills and positive emotions—much like negative emotions—are contagious. That means our EQ skills are highly dependent on the surrounding people and circumstances. The more time we spend with people who openly discuss emotions, the more skilled we become at identifying and understanding emotions. People who operate with higher emotional intelligence will also encourage our behaviors. The more we interact with empathetic people, the more empathetic we become. That is precisely what makes emotional intelligence a learned skill rather than some unalterable trait bestowed only upon a lucky few at birth.

The Journey Is Ongoing: EQ Skills Can Fluctuate

The team at TalentSmartEQ took a good look at how the collective EQ of our readers and working professionals changed over time. While we are not surprised to see that the people who we test and train successfully improve their EQ, we are interested to learn more about those who don't improve. Though people can make marked progress on their EQ skills once they get practicing, external pressures can also slow, stop, or decrease how often they are putting their EQ skills to work. Hard times of any kind—financial, familial, job-related, health-related—create more intense and often prolonged negative emotions that ultimately result in stress. In addition to the physical costs of stress, such as weight gain and heart disease, stress also taxes our mental resources. Under stress-free conditions, we can consciously devote extra effort to staying calm and collected during the trials and tribulations of everyday life. We are more confident in our abilities to handle unexpected events, and we allow our minds to overcome troublesome matters.

Unmanaged stress, however, consumes many of those mental resources. It reduces our minds to something like a state of martial law in which emotions single-handedly dictate behavior, while our rational capacities are busy trying to turn lemons into lemonade. Suddenly, a little setback in your project at work that would have been no big deal in relatively prosperous times feels more like a catastrophe than a minor nuisance. For many people, their EQ skills desert them at precisely the time when they need these skills the most—under stress. Only those with well-trained and second-nature EQ skills can effectively weather the storm.

As people work to make progress on increasing their emotional intelligence skills, we find there are three types of experiences along the way. Most people, 80%, see an increase in their EQ score after several months of practice, 3% see no change at all, and 17% see a decrease (a lower EQ score

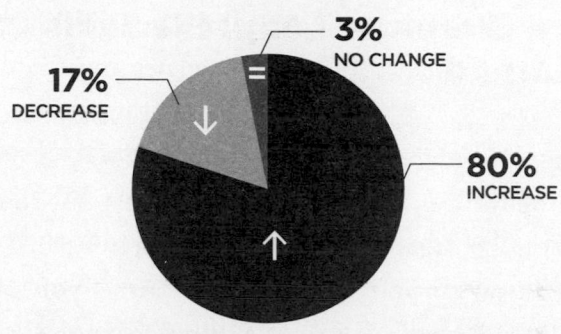

EQ Retest Scores

than their first). For people who see a decrease in their retest score, there may be two explanations. First, they may be more engaged. Now that they understand the importance of emotional intelligence, they become more aware of the moments they slip back into low EQ habits. When they take the retest, they rate themselves more realistically or hold themselves to a higher EQ standard. Second, they may hit a rough patch in life only to discover that their high EQ behaviors are less frequent than before.

Everyone's EQ journey is ongoing. Your EQ can fluctuate based on how self-aware you are or the difficulties you face. Just as you may take your foot off the pedal of a bike only to find your progress slows, you can also press the pedals and get going again. Periodically measuring your EQ scores gives you an appraisal of how much progress you are making in your efforts to master emotional intelligence skills.

Make a Quantum Leap: EQ Skills Can Be Learned

Developing emotional intelligence skills takes time, but a little conscious effort can cut that time down to a fraction of how long it would ordinarily take. Habits stem from well-traveled neural pathways in your brain, and increasing your EQ takes repeated practice until new neural connections give your brain a high EQ superhighway. Your destination is not having to spend much mental or emotional energy on what to say or do to be your best self.

Across the hundreds of thousands of learners who practice the EQ strategies in this book and then measure their progress using the Emotional Intelligence Appraisal®, we have found an average seven-point increase in their EQ scores in a three- to six-month time frame. This is more than double the increase anyone could expect from improvements and growth that happen during the normal course of life experience. The average increase in emotional intelligence scores grows to nine points for those who keep practicing several more months and then take the retest in a seven- to ten-month time frame. This means people on average make significant improvements in their EQ skills with less than a year of practice.

Seasoned working professionals frequently share with our training team that they wish they had learned about emotional

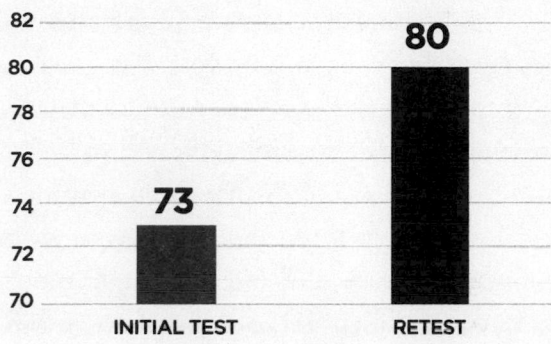

Average EQ Score from Test to Retest

intelligence earlier in life. For Gen Xers and Boomers who are midway through their careers and beyond, the wonderful news is that it is never too late to get started. People who are over 40 years old see an eight-point increase in their EQ score, on average, after practicing EQ strategies for six to nine months.

One of the signature traits of every "younger generation" is its enormous capacity to soak up new information and to acquire new skills. That means it's almost entirely up to each person to do the legwork necessary to speed up the developmental pace of their EQ. For members of Gen Y and Gen Z, the option is to either let years of experience run their course (waiting until their 50s to master their emotions) or to take their development into their own hands. If they choose to, they can start now.

With Boomers retiring sooner rather than later, talented

twenty-somethings not only can prepare themselves for leadership roles today, but they must. Those with the foresight to make the effort to train themselves to resist the temptation to speak when it won't help a situation, and to keep the lines of communication open even when upset, will be the ones tapped to fill the vacant leadership positions in tomorrow's organizations. Along with those positions will come not only better pay but also the ability to make the changes they so desperately want to see in the world.

A Competitive Advantage for Nations: EQ and Culture

Making business personal is nothing new in many cultures. In collectivistic cultures, executives ordinarily schedule dinner meetings with their staff to talk about business trends, career aspirations, and family. People expect their leaders to set an eminent example in how they make decisions, connect with others, and improve. There is genuine shame in not fulfilling these duties because staff really care.

As we discussed earlier, EQ is susceptible to cultural influence. If you grow up in a culture where emotional outbursts and careless self-gratification are not only discouraged but are also considered personally shameful, such an upbringing is going to affect the way you manage yourself and others. The question here is whether that culture promotes or prohibits emotionally intelligent behaviors.

Now, we have insights from another decade of research. An analysis of EQ and culture studies—12 studies on more than 6,000 employees—revealed that the impact of leaders' EQ on employee performance and behaviors yields statistical significance in every culture. The implications for "just business" cultures are clear: pay attention to managing emotions, or you will suffer the consequences. Whether for countries trying to protect their existing competitive advantage in the global economy or for those nations whose stars are rising, the link between EQ and outcomes such as job satisfaction, performance, and economic prosperity cannot be overestimated.

> **The implications for "just business" cultures are clear: pay attention to managing emotions or suffer the consequences.**

There's an old Chinese proverb that says, "Give a man a pole and he'll catch a fish a week. Tell him what bait to use, and he'll catch a fish a day. Show him how and where to fish, and he'll have fish to eat for a lifetime." The flip side to that proverb is that the person without a pole, without bait, and without knowledge of the *how* and the *where* runs a serious risk of famine. Similarly, emotionally ignorant people with little understanding of how and where emotions affect their lives will have an exceedingly difficult time reeling in success. On the other hand, those who use the right tools and strategies for harnessing their emotions put themselves in a position to prosper. That same truth applies to individuals, organizations, and even entire communities and countries.

Closing Thoughts: EQ and the Future

While the sum total of these findings is encouraging, these discoveries also act as a stern warning. For every person setting out to increase their EQ, keep in mind that emotional intelligence is a skill set that can be unlearned during periods of stress or hardship. For those who are in leadership positions today or who desire a leadership role in the future, learn how to manage your moods constructively with the strategies in this book, or the performance of the people you lead can suffer.

The important point is to keep at it. Just as you can work hard to lose weight over the summer only to pack those pounds on again over the winter holidays, you can sharpen your EQ skills only to see them go dull again. That is precisely why we recommend reading this book, putting your new knowledge into action, and reviewing these skill development strategies at least once a year.

You wouldn't expect to forever master the game of golf or playing the piano after practicing for six months and then quitting, would you? The same is true with EQ skill development. If you let up and stop consciously practicing these skills, somewhere down the road, you will almost certainly allow tough circumstances to overpower you. You will slide right back into those old bad habits. These hard-earned skills can be lost almost as easily as they were gained, and with them the higher performance, stronger relationships, and better decisions you've come to enjoy.

DISCUSSION QUESTIONS FOR READING GROUPS

Discussing EQ will help you bridge the learning-doing gap. Use these questions to start a meaningful dialogue and build your understanding of how the four EQ skills apply in daily living.

1. How many members in the group were familiar with the term "emotional intelligence" before reading *Emotional Intelligence 2.0*?

2. For those who had never heard of EQ before, what's the most important thing you discovered after reading *Emotional Intelligence 2.0*?

3. For those who were familiar with EQ before reading the book, what's the most important thing you discovered?

4. Have you ever felt an emotional hijacking similar to Butch Connor's during his run-in with the shark?

5. What are the physical symptoms you experience with emotion? An example might be your face turns red when you're angry.

6. What are a few fundamental changes you might like to make now that you know change can happen at a physical level? What would you like to train your brain to do?

7. What's one experience that stands out for you in learning to recognize or manage your emotions? What about learning to recognize what other people are feeling?

8. In your job, how are emotions dealt with? Is there anything covered in the book that will help you in the next six months at work? How about next week?

9. How are EQ skills visible in current events today? Discuss politicians, celebrities, athletes, etc.

10. Can you think of any historical figures or events that were influenced by either poor management or excellent management of emotions?

11. Only 36% of people are able to identify their emotions accurately as they happen. Why do you suppose this is the case? How might someone get better at this?

12. Groups that decide to take the online *Emotional Intelligence Appraisal*® test before meeting can bring their results and discuss them as follows:

    a. Without sharing specific numbers, which EQ skill score was your highest?

    b. Which EQ skill score was your lowest? Which strategies will you practice to improve this skill?

13. What will make practicing EQ skills most challenging for you?

14. What would you like to know from the other people in the group about how they:

    • Work on being more self-aware?

    • Self-manage?

    • Read feelings or emotions in other people?

    • Manage relationships?

15. Consider any facts mentioned in the book that you found fascinating and discuss them as a group, for example:

- Emotions are contagious.

- Your EQ can fluctuate due to influences such as stress or hardship.

- EQ skills can be learned.

- EQ behaviors are susceptible to cultural influence.

NOTES

The Journey

The story of Butch Connor's shark attack comes from a highly entertaining book of true stories edited by Paul Diamond, *Surfing's Greatest Misadventures: Dropping In on the Unexpected*, (Seattle: Casagrande Press, 2006). Online at: https://casagrandepress.com/surfings-greatest-misadventures-dropping-in-on-the-unexpected/. Another account of the incident from Demian Bulwa (2004, May 31). Surfer goes toe-to-toe with shark. *The San Francisco Chronicle*.

W.L. Payne coined the term emotional intelligence: "A study of emotion: Developing emotional intelligence: Self integration; relating to fear, pain and desire." Doctoral thesis, The Union Institute, Cincinnati, OH (1988).

Seminal emotional intelligence research contributing to the term's spread in popularity: from Yale University: Jack Mayer, et al., "Perceiving affective content in ambiguous visual stimuli: A component of emotional intelligence." *Journal of Personality Assessment*, 54 (1990). A second study linking emotional intelligence to success: Jack Mayer and Peter Salovey, "The intelligence of emotional intelligence." *Intelligence,* 17 (1993). A third linking it to well-being:

J. Mayer and A. Stevens, "An emerging understanding of the reflective (meta) experience of mood." *Journal of Research in Personality,* 28 (1994).

Gibbs, Nancy (1995, October 2). The EQ Factor. *Time* magazine.

Travis Bradberry and Jean Greaves, *The Emotional Intelligence Quick Book*, (New York: Simon & Schuster, 2005).

The Big Picture

The feelings table has been reproduced and modified with the permission of the original creator, Julia West. The table was initially featured on her former website for science fiction writers.

Emotional hijacking is a term first introduced in a book by Daniel Goleman, *Emotional Intelligence: Why It Can Matter More Than IQ*, (New York: Bantam, 2005).

The tendency of low EQ individuals to catch up to their colleagues' higher scores after an EQ skill development initiative is from Neil M. Ashkanasy, "The case for emotional intelligence in workgroups" Symposium presentation at the annual conference of the Society for Industrial and Organizational Psychology (April, 2001).

Emotional intelligence subsuming 33 other leadership skills is seen in Dr. Travis Bradberry, *Self-Awareness: The Hidden Driver of Success and Satisfaction*, (New York: Putnam, 2009).

The connection between EQ and job performance and the tendency for high performers to be high in EQ is from Travis Bradberry and Jean Greaves, *The Emotional Intelligence Quick Book*, (New York: Simon & Schuster, 2005).

The link between EQ and annual salary is seen in Bradberry, T., Tasler, N. "Increasing Your Salary with Emotional Intelligence" *TalentSmartEQ* (2009). Available online at http://www.talentsmarteq.com/articles.

What Emotional Intelligence Looks Like: Understanding The Four Skills

The emotional intelligence model that groups the four skills (self-awareness, self-management, social awareness, and relationship management) into the larger categories of personal and social competence is from Goleman, Boyatzis, and McKee, *Primal Leadership: Realizing the Power of Emotional Intelligence*, (Boston: Harvard Business School Press, 2002).

The link between self-awareness skills and job performance is seen in Travis Bradberry, *Self-Awareness: The Hidden Driver of Success and Satisfaction*, (New York: Putnam, 2009).

More than 70% of the people we tested have difficulty handling stress comes from Travis Bradberry and Jean Greaves, *The Emotional Intelligence Quick Book*, (New York: Simon & Schuster, 2005).

The importance of putting your needs on hold to get results is seen in Ayduk, O. & Mischel, W., "When Smart People Behave Stupidly: Reconciling inconsistencies in social-emotional intelligence." Chapter in *Why Smart People Can Be So Stupid*, Edited by Robert J. Sternberg, (New Haven: Yale University Press, 2002).

Digging In

Studies of brain plasticity: T. P. Pons, et al., "Massive cortical reorganization after sensory deafferentation in adult macaques, *Science* (252). N. Jain, (1997), "Deactivation and reactivation of somatosensory cortex is accompanied by reductions in GABA straining, *Somatosens Mot. Res*, 8 (347-354). D. Borsook, et al. (1998), "Acute plasticity in the human somatosensory cortex following amputation, *NeuroReport*, 9 (1013-1017). Katri Cornelleson (2003), "Adult brain plasticity influenced by anomia treatment." *Journal of Cognitive Neuroscience*, 15 (3).

Studies from The Harvard Medical School examining changes in brain structure: B.A. van der Kolk. "The body keeps the score: Memory and the emerging psychobiology of post traumatic stress." *Harvard Review of Psychiatry*, 1, 253265 (1994), and B.A. van der Kolk et al., "Dissociation, somatization, and affect dysregulation: the complexity of adaptation of trauma." *American Journal of Psychiatry*, 153, 83-93 (1996).

The benchmark study demonstrating changes in EQ six years after an EQ skill development initiative is seen in Richard Boyatzis, et al. in *Innovation in Professional Education: Steps on a Journey from Teaching to Learning*, (San Francisco: Jossey-Bass, 1995).

Self-Management Strategies

Self-management strategy #3, Make Your Goals Public, considers research from Francis Hesselbein et al. *The Leader of the Future*, (San Francisco: Jossey-Bass, 1997).

Self-management strategy #7, Smile and Laugh More, discusses the benefit of smiling according to findings from: Soussignan, R. (2002). Duchenne smile, emotional experience, and autonomic reactivity: A test of the facial feedback hypothesis. *Journal of Personality and Social Psychology*, 2, 52-74.

Self-management strategy #9, Take Control of Your Self-Talk, discusses the number of thoughts an average person has in one day according to findings from: The National Science Foundation (www.nsf.gov).

The importance of self-talk in managing your emotions is seen in: Fletcher, J.E. (1989). "Physiological Foundations of Intrapersonal Communication." In Roberts & Watson (Eds.), *Intrapersonal Communication Processes*, (188-202). New Orleans: Spectra. Grainger, R.D. (1991). "The Use—and Abuse—of Negative Thinking." *American Journal of Nursing*, 91(8), 13-14. Korba, R. (1989). "The Cognitive Psychophysiology of Inner Speech." In Roberts & Watson (Eds.), *Intrapersonal Communication Processes*, (217-242). New Orleans: Spectra. Levine, B.H., *Your Body Believes Every Word You Say: The Language of the Body/Mind Connection*, (Boulder Creek: Aslan, 1991).

Self-management strategy #10, Visualize Yourself Succeeding, discusses the power of visualization according to findings from: Kosslyn, S. M.; Ganis, G.; Thompson, W. L. (2007). Mental imagery and the human brain. In: *Progress in Psychological Science Around the World, Vol. 1: Neural, Cognitive and Developmental Issues*, Jing Q., Rosenweig M. R., d'Ydewalle G., Zhang H., Chen H.-C., Zhang K., ed. (New York: Psychology Press), 195–209.

Social Awareness Strategies

Strategy #2, Watch Body Language discusses research on reading emotions, facial expressions, and body language from Dr. Paul Ekman, *Emotions Revealed: Recognizing Faces and Feelings to Improve Communication and Emotional Life*, (New York: Henry Holt & Company, 2007).

Relationship Management Strategies

Relationship management strategy #4, Remember the Little Things That Pack a Punch, discusses the research regarding the decline of manners in America and employee opinions about manners in the workplace according to findings from: Public Agenda Research Group, reported on ABCNEWS.com, April 3, 2002 and ABCNEWS/World Tonight Poll, May 1999.

For research on repairing conversations, John Gottman and Robert W. Levenson, "A Two-Factor Model for Predicting When a Couple Will Divorce: Exploratory Analyses Using 14-Year Longitudinal Data," *Family Process* 41 (2002): 83–96.

Epilogue

Emotional contagion is analyzed in two Leadership Quarterly articles: "Emotionality and Leadership: Taking Stock of the Past Decade of Research," by Rashimah Rajah, Zhaoli Song, and Richard D. Arvey, 22 (2011), 11071119; and "The Emotional Link: Leadership and the Role of Implicit and Explicit Emotional Contagion Processes Across Multiple Organizational Levels," by Eugene Y. J. Tee. 26 (2015), 654-670.

The article, "Can Emotional Intelligence be Trained? A Meta-analytical Investigation," by Victoria Mattingly and Kurt Kraiger, Human Resources Management Review 29 (2019) 140-155, concludes EQ skills are trainable. Across 76 research studies between 2000-2016, pre-post and treatment-control group designs all found positive effects, regardless of gender.

For an analysis of research on EQ and cultural influences, Chao Miao, Ronald H. Humphrey and Shanshan Qian, "A Cross-cultural Meta-analysis of How Leader Emotional Intelligence Influences Subordinate Task Performance and Organnizational Citizenship Behavior," Journal of World Business 53 (2018), 463-474.

EQ retest and age-related scores from the *Emotional Intelligence Appraisal®* are compiled from a test-retest data set for 1,879 learners who completed the retest in 2020 between three to eleven months after completing their first assessment. For further discussion of EQ data trends, visit www.TalentSmartEQ.com/EQtrends.

EQ RESOURCE GUIDE

For more information about EQ and tools to assist you in teaching others about EQ, review the resources in the following pages, and contact TalentSmartEQ at www.talentsmarteq.com/contact. TalentSmartEQ also offers complimentary EQ resources, including articles, white papers, webinars, and the Better EQ newsletter covering the latest in workplace learning. You can subscribe for free at www.talentsmarteq.com.

Take Your EQ to the Next Level

You've learned how emotional intelligence can help you get where you want to go. **Now it's time to continue your learning journey.**

Our clients find that continued practice, training, and coaching can increase their EQ by an average of 7 points over 6-9 months.

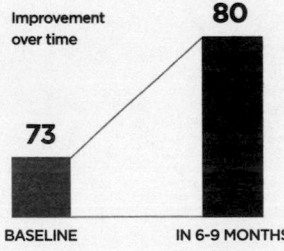

Improvement over time

73

80

BASELINE

IN 6-9 MONTHS

The TalentSmartEQ® **Emotional Intelligence Appraisal®** assessment included in this book shows you how to harness the power of EQ at work and in life.

Use the unique code in the sealed envelope at the back of this book to take the assessment to:

▼ **LEARN** what behaviors are **lifting you up, or holding you back**

▼ **UNCOVER** the strategies most personally relevant to **increasing your EQ**

▼ **TURN** insight into immediate **action and lasting improvement**

You can start practicing your personalized strategies right away. Use this resource guide to explore additional ways to accelerate your development through continued practice and training.

TalentSmartEQ

Take EQ to Your Organization

EQ development isn't just for Individuals. It's also a foundation for addressing critical challenges your organization faces including: engaging employees, driving productivity, and navigating change. Stronger EQ skills in the workplace provide a competitive advantage by improving outcomes that are critical to your organization's performance and culture:

▼ **HIGHER PRODUCTIVITY**

▼ **INCREASED ENGAGEMENT**

▼ **IMPROVED COLLABORATION**

▼ **ABILITY TO NAVIGATE CHANGE AND UNCERTAINTY**

▼ **MORE EFFECTIVE LEADERSHIP**

▼ **MARKET-DRIVEN INNOVATION**

▼ **GREATER RESILIENCE**

Consider these gains our clients have realized from utilizing our programs.

Leaders at one of the largest US not-for-profit health systems experienced a:

93% improvement in their ability to handle conflict effectively.

57% improvement in their ability to deal effectively with change.

54% improvement in their ability to communicate clearly and effectively.

Engineers at a Fortune 200 defense contractor experienced a:

40% improvement in their ability to handle change effectively.

26% improvement in the quality of their relationships with their coworkers.

WORLD'S #1 PROVIDER OF EMOTIONAL INTELLIGENCE

Why TalentSmartEQ

TalentSmartEQ has spent over 20 years focused on bringing emotional intelligence research and skill development to the world.

**2 Million+
Assessments**

**75% Fortune
500 Served**

**2 Million+
Books Sold**

**35+ Countries
25+ Languages**

We have flexible tools to help individuals, teams, and entire organizations using proven and practical approaches that meet your learners where they are.

▼ **WE CAN
TRAIN YOUR
EMPLOYEES**

▼ **WE CAN
TRAIN YOUR
TRAINERS**

▼ **WE CAN
COACH YOUR
LEADERS**

TalentSmartEQ

What Our Customers Have Shared

Learn more about TalentSmartEQ's emotional intelligence solutions, and how EQ development can give your organization a competitive advantage.

"

Best training our company has ever had. I will never view a customer the same. This has helped with my relationships at home and my life.
– Program Participant from a National Furniture Retailer

Invaluable in identifying strengths and opportunities to improve your EQ. It helped me to apply direct strategies, improving my approach to work and my relationships each day.
– Program Participant at a Global Financial Company

One of the most valuable events in my professional training life...Thank you!
– Certified Trainer from an Energy and Utilities Organization

This program relates to real-life work experiences. It resonates with all types of personalities and employees, and it's totally universal across all levels and functions.
– Executive at a Multi-national Retail Client

The best, most impactful class our team has had the pleasure to teach!
– Development Leader at a Division of a National Defense Organization

"

Visit **www.talentsmarteq.com/eqtrends** for complimentary access to the latest insights and research on emotional intelligence.

WORLD'S #1 PROVIDER OF EMOTIONAL INTELLIGENCE